You Are NEVER ALONE

by Rita Aasen

Translated from Norwegian to American English by INGUNN OESTBY

January 2012

Copyright © 2013 by Rita Aasen

You are never alone
by Rita Aasen

Printed in the United States of America

ISBN 9781628396966

All rights reserved solely by the author. The author guarantees all contents are original and do not infringe upon the legal rights of any other person or work. No part of this book may be reproduced in any form without the permission of the author. The views expressed in this book are not necessarily those of the publisher.

Unless otherwise indicated, Bible quotations are taken from the New International Version 1984, unless anything else has been mentioned.

www.xulonpress.com

TABLE OF CONTENTS

Words in time of need: 13
- He Chooses
- The Honey Tune
- God's Way
- The One Who Refreshes Others…
- Thanks For the Book
- Children and Poetry
- The Atheist and the Nativity Gospel
- The Lord Your God Will Walk With You
- Poetry for the Entire Village
- Be Faithful and Patient
- The Cross of the Three Nails
- Tired After a Mission
- Clare's Song
- Benjamin

Forgive us our debts, as we also have forgiven our debtors. . .37
- Grace isn't Cheap
- God's Amazing Gift: Forgiveness
- Do You Love Me?

I will instruct you and teach you in the way you should go . . .49
- The Biggest Crown
- An Extra Flight
- Three Things Within an Hour
- "Enlarge the place of your tent" Isaiah 54:2
- A Willing Heart

He Knows our Needs 61
- The Flour Jar and the Oil Mug
- Pay From the Lord
- Angel and Salary
- Laser Printer
- Printing Cards in Faith
- New Flatware
- Closed Doors
- Do You Always Receive Answers to Prayers?

Fear not, for I am with you 77
- Butterflies and Wandering
- Light for the Walk Home –
- No One Will Make You Afraid
- I Fear Not For The Night
- Loved and Unique
- All Your Children
- Sow in Weakness
- The Lord Will Fight For you
- Jesus is With you in the Furnace
- In the Valley of Death
- A Disciple's Tongue

"The Lord sustains them on their sickbed and restores them from their bed of illness" Psalm 41:3 95
- Wherever You are, There Jesus Will Be
- Now Go
- Stand Firm!
- Waiting For the Lord
- "Whoever dwells in the shelter of the Most High" Psalm 91:1
- God is Able to Bless You Abundantly
- Cry Unto Me
- Messianic Believers
- The Two Jars

"… in quietness and trust is your strength" Isaiah 30:15 113
- "He giveth, and giveth, and giveth again"
- "…he carries them close to his heart" Isaiah 40:11

Table of Contents

- A Lesson Learned
- Give Yourself Time For Food and Rest
-

Therefore I tell you, do not worry about you life, what you will eat or drink..." Matthew 6:25..........................125
- Abundance on the Stairs
- "Hardangerlefser"
- Cake with the Coffee

With Jesus in Hungary...............................131
- Eger in Hungary
- "I've been waiting for this"
- "...do not let your hands hang limp" Zephaniah 3:16
- "... he leads me beside quiet waters" Psalm 23:2

In God We Trust....................................139
- In God's Hand
- An American Bible
- I know where I'm going
- How do you get to Heaven?

PREFACE

This new book by Rita Aasen is another pearl. My reading of this book has rendered me happy and grateful. Her testimonies speak vividly about a Father and a Savior who cares about His children. He listens and sees. Rita tells about answers to prayer regarding both small and great things. Often God calls His children to be His messengers. When in need of a word of encouragement, it happens that Rita gets a text message or a phone call. Not seldom, the answer to prayer from God is confirmed by many receiving the same word from the Bible. Rita's stories impart that God is a God who is present.

Her personal relationship and love to Jesus run as a thread through her testimonies. When I was reading the story about "The Two Jars," I met a priest who had great experience within spiritual guidance and retreat work. He read the story. He was moved, and told me that he looked forward to this book arriving in the bookstore.

Now it's here. Rita has pleased many with her previous books. Many have received help. The books speak to our hearts. As will this book.

Stig Magne Heitmann
Director of Open Doors, Norway

" … in every situation, by prayer and petition … present your requests to God."

Again Rita Aasen has given us a book with faith-strengthening testimonies that God is a God who listens to prayers.

When I read through the manuscript, I had to ask myself: What is the reason that Rita experiences so many more answers to prayers than the rest of us? I think the answer is simple: She places *all things* before God in her prayers. She *expects* that our heavenly Father is interested in everything, from the little everyday-life needs to the great special challenges we may be facing. And she *waits* till the Lord answers, whether the answer is yes or no.

We so easily make our own plans, and then pray to the Lord to bless what we have come up with. Rita asks for God's plan, for that is when she knows that she has the Lord's blessing with her.

But this is no glorification theology: Just pray and believe and everything will be all right. Rather, it is a theology of honesty that she brings forth. She tells about an illness that she was not cured from, but she is given strength to live with it and thus be capable of accomplishing what she was called to do. She tells about her battle, doubt, opposition, betrayal, fatigue, and despondency. However, it's because of this that her testimony is so trustworthy. For the Lord is with her through it all. Thus, the book's many testimonies strongly emphasize how we are only pottery jars but still containing a great treasure.

It is also moving to read about all the people who have listened to the Lord's voice and been obedient to do what the Lord has called them to do, everything from sending a little greeting either as a text message or in a letter, to coming with gifts, whether these were bread, cakes, laser printers or great amounts of money. This challenges and inspires us to follow this example.

Thanks to Rita and all of you who have been mentioned both with and without names, for the testimonies that we have a Father in heaven who knows what we need, and who cares about us!

Oddvar Soevik
Region leader of Normisjon region Agder*

* *Normisjon region Agder* is a voluntary and independent mission agency within the Lutheran Church of Norway. It focuses on fellowship and mission both in Norway and beyond.

PREFACE

It can be hard to accept how life turned out. In Isaiah 43:2, it is written: The reality I've met several times through conversations and during intercession has been marked by aggravated sexual assaults, violence, assaults, and abuse. Children, youth and young adults die because of illness or in accidents. The pain is overwhelming.

I've met pedophiles, criminals, heterosexuals, homosexuals, everyday heroes, tired, sick and dying people – and those wanting to live longer. I've met faith heroes, people in sorrow, alcoholics and drug addicts. I've met those who chose to have an abortion, and those who chose to keep the baby. Those who handled the parent role, and those who didn't. I've met people who's lonely as human; the anxious, the eager and aspiring; the manipulator, the assailant, and the pure in heart and pure in conduct. Jealousy, envy, hatred and bitterness can influence life and surroundings, causing everything to fall apart. There have been many encounters in my life and in the room of counseling. When Jesus was born, angelic proclamation sounded. However, the heavenly song was no guarantee against persecution.

H.E. Wisloeff once put it this way: "The Devil uses times of trouble to make us disheartened and weak. God uses them to make us undaunted and strong. Thus, He is always closer when the fire of times of trouble encircles us. And never is His power more effective."

I myself struggle with poor health. Loss of health can cause sorrow and a feeling that life has been reduced. It can cause anxiety for not being accepted by the environment and the society. Because you don't perform in a way "the others" do. The feeling of being a burden is hard. You can easily fall into the ditch where you convince yourself that your value is connected to what you perform. A friend of mine with cancer once said: "What really weakens the strengths is all these extra gates the sick have to open and close. The healthy don't have to do this."

My way through the fire has been to stay close to God's word. This has been my lifeline, giving power and strength. Whatever I've met or have been exposed to, the Word has been my counselor through it all. I have many questions and many things I don't understand, but the Word has given me wisdom in my inexperience, ignorance and walk. It has given me joy in my heart. Hope and comfort through days when nothing seemed to either live or grow.

I have experienced that the heart and the intellect are two different things. I've chosen to do what is written in Proverbs 3:5: *"Trust in the Lord with all your heart and lean not on your own understanding…"* This has been sufficient. This has carried me through.

There have also been days when I've caught glimpses of Him who sees, He who was born into our world of pain. He who is with us through everything – whether we see it or we don't. For we are never ever alone, nor left by ourselves.

God is mighty to save us out of persecution, times of trouble, illness and accidents, but if He doesn't do it, I'll still put my faith in Him alone.

In Daniel chapter 3 we can read about Daniel's three friends and the furnace. They met persecution because of their faith. They said: *"If we are thrown into the blazing furnace, the God we serve is able to deliver us from it, and he will deliver us from Your Majesty's hand. But even if he does not, we want you to know, Your Majesty, that we will not serve your gods or worship the image of gold you have set up"* (Daniel 3:17-18). This resulted in them being tied up and thrown into the furnace to die.

The ropes that tied them were burned away in the furnace.

But perhaps you ask: Why do we have to go through the furnace when all we've done is to walk with the Lord? If we must go, we never walk alone there either. For there were four men in the furnace. One looked like a son of the gods, who was with them all the time. It was the Lord Jesus Christ, God's only begotten son. They were never alone.

Preface

Whether the Lord saves us from persecution, this world's times of trouble, or illness while we're living on earth, He is with us. If He doesn't save us from this while we're here, He is still the God who loves us, and who walks with us all the way home. He is with us all days and all kinds of days. Whether I see His answer or not, I will rely on Him. For He is with me.

This book is my little testimony. I can't answer all the whys. You won't find any human who can. But I can testify about what I've seen and experienced in the many days of my life when I've chosen to trust Him who is the Word itself, the Lord Jesus Christ. I've seen that the one who seeks refuge in Him is never, ever alone when the fire comes. Maybe you don't see Him or experience that He is with you, but He is, for the Word says so.

When I was working on my first book with testimonies, *In God's Hand*, almost everyone who had been mentioned wanted to remain anonymous. Together with the publishing company it was then decided that no names were to be mentioned. During the work on this book, more chose to be mentioned with names or where they were from. Again, some remained anonymous this time, and I respect that. They've all expressed joy for being able to participate. I thank them all.

I hope these simple testimonies will point at Jesus so that they leave a fragrance of Him and Him alone. All the Bible references in this English version of my book are taken from the New International Version 1984, unless anything else has been mentioned.

I especially want to thank web-pastor of the Christian radio broadcaster *Norea,* Asbjoern Kvalbein, priest and region leader in Normisjon, Oddvar Soevik, and secretary-general of Open Doors in Norway, Stig Magne Heitmann, for having read through and come up with good advice regarding the manuscript.

Kristiansand, January 2012
Rita Aasen

WORDS IN TIME
OF NEED

He chooses

I began to doubt whether I should continue to write more books. Time had showed me that some people didn't like what I was writing. One day I met some people I knew who hadn't much pleasant to say to me. Instead, they spoke contemptibly of how I was testifying through my books. This didn't improve when they heard that the Christian Norwegian publisher, *Lunde Forlag,* had asked me to write a new book on walking with Jesus. Hard words fell from people whom I didn't expect such. I felt betrayed, and many thoughts formed.

At home I cried out to God: *How do You view this?* When I went to bed that night, I felt how despondency settled in me. But early the next morning, a text message ticked in on my cell phone from another lady. She wrote of how she wanted to greet me with the same words that the Lord spoke to Joshua, the son of Nun, about his walk in favor. He said: *"I will never leave you nor forsake you."* (Joshua 1:5).

Two hours later, a greeting from another lady ticked in with the words from 1Corinthians 1:18-31, where God speaks to us about how He chooses what at first looks like nothing. In verses 27-29 it is written: *"But God chose the foolish things of the world to shame the wise; God chose the weak things of the world to shame the strong. God chose the lowly things of this world and the despised things—and the things that are not—to nullify the things that are, so that no one may boast before him."*

It felt good to take this in. It encouraged me to continue the walk. For this very day I was going to give a Bible to an atheist who had read one of my books, someone who ever since then I'd had several conversations with. We had now reached a point in which the person had said that she wished to get to know the Jesus I had testified about. On my way home, another text message ticked in, this time from a lady I had been in service with earlier. She wanted to remind me of how the fruit tree is a good picture on the walk with the Lord – the gardener always prunes the branch and trims a branch that bears fruit. So do not be discouraged! The Lord will never leave your side.

Neither of these three knew my situation. It was a wondrous day. I decided to continue writing.

It is often the accusations made by ourselves or others that create our circumstances. What remains important here is always what we do about this – whether we go to Jesus with it or we don't. He will never grow weary of us. Nor does He abandon us. God is merciful. He will complete the work He has begun in us. He is the one who says: *"Never will I leave you; never will I forsake you."*

The Honey tune

If you experience coldness from other humans over time, it does something to you. Then the rescue can be to walk next to Jesus and learn from Him. One day I felt the rejection and coldness extra strongly, and I felt it was difficult to forgive. I said to Jesus that I needed His help to understand why I had to go through this. The same day a letter came in the mail. The writer was a woman from a place in the middle of Setesdal (a valley and a traditional district in the eastern part of South Norway). A lady in Valle wrote that she had been reminded to give me a story she hoped would fit. In the letter, a story called the *The Honey Tune* was enclosed. In amazement I sat down and read:

"It is said one of the world's greatest violinists before the Second World War, the Polish-born Bronislaw Hubermann, was – despite his virtuosity – not content. He sought for something in his play that was called 'the honey tune' – a special vibration with a characteristic softness and touch. But he didn't manage to find it. Then the war came. Since Hubermann was half-Jewish, his whole family was sent to concentration camps and died there. He himself managed to flee to Switzerland and later to England. There he was asked to play, but he replied: 'I can't do it. My grief is too much. I've lost my whole family.' However, they continued begging him until he finally agreed to play one sonata only.

"Royal Albert Hall, which seats ten thousand, was sold out to a full house. Hubermann gazed out at the hopeful audience before he raised his bow and began playing. While playing he envisioned in his inner eye his mother and father, his siblings, the gas chambers and the suffering. He forgot about the ten thousand – and then he noticed that he had something in his playing that he never before had accomplished to bring out: the honey tune. It wound up with him playing for more than two hours, and when the concert was over the whole crowd rose to their feet. But they didn't applaud. They just stood there and wept.

"The next day the newspaper wrote: 'The review bow and scrape for the perfection. In the suffering he found the tune he had longed for all his life.'"

For a long time I just sat with the letter in my hands. The story about Hubermann held a deep knowledge – greater than our lives. It might be that God also will meet you where you do not expect to find Him. God desires to bring forth this "honey tune" in us, so that people will meet another reality. A meeting with Jesus Christ. Obedience is the way. In Hebrews 5:8 it says: *"Although he was a son, he learned obedience from what he suffered."*

Jesus holds truth and healing. He gives forgiveness for your life. With Him you will receive knowledge about the true love. Perpetually He proved on the Cross of Calvary what a formidable, propitiatory sacrifice He brought about for all sin and all injustice. With Him you will see that you yourself are forgiven by grace alone. With Jesus you have a choice – you can forgive. Most of all, for your own sake, hand over your case to Him who will judge with righteousness. "*...I will repay,*" says the Lord. (Rom 12:19). Then you shall be released from your inner prison. In a Norwegian song we sing: "The Name of Jesus": "...for this name all hatred must recede." In Luke 23:33-34 it is written about He who lived what He had learned: *"When they came to the place called the Skull, they crucified him there, along with the criminals—one on his right, the* *other on his left. Jesus said, 'Father, forgive them, for they do not know what they are doing.'"*

God's Way

When eaglets learn to fly, they are flung out of the nest. At high altitude. If the eagle mom hadn't caught them on her wings and carried them safely to the nest again, that would have been the end for the eaglets.

When the road you are guided through doesn't always make sense, the questions arrive in succession. Not always do we get the answers we desire. However, over time it well might be that we will see the answer arriving despite it all. Sometimes, we are confronted with encounters and events that we preferably would have steered clear of, if we were given the choice.

I was going to a meeting that I didn't want to be part of. But life isn't always this way that you can avoid being nudged out of the safe nest and out in free flight, directed towards the ground. I went to the Father in prayer. Could I please be excused from attending this meeting? And what was His perspective on the matter?

Then a text message ticked in on my cell phone from a lady who knew nothing about the situation I was facing. She wrote that she only wanted to greet me with: *"The Lord carries you on His wings. He protects you. Under His wings you shall find shelter."* I was so happy for this greeting and thanked God for it. At the same time, I knew that I had to survive this meeting. There was no way out for me. Not long after, a priest from Soegne (a town located in South Norway), Jan Pedersen called me. He just wanted to tell me that Jesus always walks before us. He had been preaching about this the day before, and had felt that he had to remind me about this. He didn't know about the circumstances I was facing, but he hoped it could be of help. It turned out to be a blessed conversation that day – and a new thanks to God.

We do not always know what to pray for, but the Holy Spirit comes to help us here as well. The mother of the Church Father St. Augustine prayed a lot for her son, both for his childhood and his adult age. If only he could be saved! But Augustine led a debauched and wild life.

One day he wanted to go to Italy. His mother then cried and prayed to God that He had to stop him from going. But Augustine left – and was actually saved in Italy. God saw the meaning behind the prayer.

Whenever we face a situation that we are begging to be spared from, and God leads us through it, this is what we really are: *"like an eagle that stirs up its nest and hovers over its young, that spreads its wings to catch them and carries them aloft. The LORD alone led him; no foreign god was with him. He made him ride on the heights of the land and fed him with the fruit of the fields. He nourished him with honey from the rock, and with oil from the flinty crag..."* (Deuteronomy 32:11-13)

Those situations when we are *"pushed out of the nest"* can be as if hitting the hardest rock, but from it oil will come, says the Word. Oil from the Lord. From Him who *"anoints my head with oil; my cup overflows"* (Psalm 23:5).

The one who refreshes others...

When we are down, feel like a failure, and believe we need to be cheered up, we tend to seek the Lord, hoping to receive some encouragement from Him. What we often seem to forget, however, is that the Lord's thoughts are greater than our own. In Isaiah 55:8-9, He says: *"For my thoughts are not your thoughts, neither are your ways my ways,"* declares the Lord. *"As the heavens are higher than the earth, so are my ways higher than your ways and my thoughts than your thoughts."*

One day as I was feeling down, I prayed for encouragement. But the only thing that came to mind was that I should encourage another lady whom I had worked together with earlier. This was not what I had expected the Lord to reply with, but I really cared for this lady. For that reason, I sat down and asked the Lord to remind me on what I should say to her. Then I sent her my greeting, and not long after I got a reply that this had meant a lot to her. This was also encouraging for me.

That very day I got a greeting from another lady who had no knowledge on these matters whatsoever. She wrote: "The true value of a good deed rests in the love that inspired it. Nobody here in this world is a failure if that person can ease the burden of another."

Indeed, His thoughts are higher than our own. The peace that transcends all understanding came as a gift. The verse in Proverbs about refreshing others then came to me. *"A generous person will prosper; whoever refreshes others will be refreshed"* (Proverbs 11:25). Indeed, His thoughts are higher than our own in this as well.

Thanks for the book

Where I gave a speech for the Interior Seamen's Mission. The books I have written were sold here as well. Among other titles was *In God's Hand*.

Almost a month later, a lady called me, telling me that she got hold of this book after I had been there. By now she had read it three times. It turned out that it felt so good for her, because she was ill and had turned away from Jesus. "Without this book I'm not sure how I would have made it through it all. It helped bring me back to Jesus. So now I'm a Christian again," she said.

There were a lot of things that had spoken to her, but it was one chapter in particular that had struck her. It was the one I had written about how I had been given a cross-shaped stone by my heavenly Father when I asked for it. She herself had once found a heart-shaped stone on a beach in Denmark when she was deeply in despair and facing a difficult situation. The memory re-appeared and she was so grateful for yet again coming to Jesus, to Him who is *"the pioneer and the perfecter of faith"* (Hebrews 12:2).

She turned to Him as it is written in Micah 7:19: *"You will again have compassion on us; you will tread our sins underfoot and hurl all our iniquities into the depths of the sea."* She turned to Him who never stops loving, Him who searches till He finds you, so that He can guide you all the way home. *"For you were like sheep going astray, but now you have returned to the Shepherd and Overseer of your souls"* (1 Peter 2:25).

Children and Poetry

When I write poetry, I never have children in mind as a target group, rather it is youth and adults I have in mind. However, when I had published the book *He Walks Before You,* I received a response that was both a surprise and a delight.

Astrid Pedersen, a lady living in Soegne, a little place on the Southern coast of Norway, told me she had given the book to a friend as a present. Her friend had sat down and read the book immediately upon receiving it. What she had read had stirred her so strongly that she later called and told Astrid about it. But, she said, another strange thing happened with this book when her ten-year-old grandchild stopped by.

This child was a boy who suffered from a rare disease that meant he wouldn't live to grow up. He knew this and they talked openly about it in his family. This disease caused him to be very jittery, something that was troublesome for he himself and a challenge for the surroundings.

One evening when grandma was going to ease the parents by looking after him, the boy was very jittery. The plan was that he should stay overnight with her. When his parents had left, she sat down next to his bed and began to read from the poetry book she had received as a gift. The boy became completely still – just lay there and listened attentively. Grandma could state with astonishment that he hadn't been this calm for many years.

Heaven had become a place he knew he wanted to go to, before the others – this they had talked much about. Jesus would be there, too. For this reason, Heaven had become a safe place for him. She read the entire book for the boy, and he was calm and still the whole time. This had become a precious and sacred moment for them both, grandma said.

"At that time the disciples came to Jesus and asked, 'Who, then, is the greatest in the kingdom of heaven?' He called a little child to him, and placed the child among them. And he said: 'Truly I tell you, unless you change and become like little children, you will never enter the kingdom of heaven. Therefore, whoever takes the lowly position of this child is the greatest in the kingdom of heaven'" (Matt 18:1-4).

The Atheist and the Nativity Gospel

In Isaiah 35 it is written: *"No wayfaring person, not even the fool shall go astray."* God has prepared the way to Heaven so clearly that not even the least talented will go astray. If you follow Jesus, who is the Way home to our heavenly Father, some might think of you as a fool. But if you walk on that road, you shall become wise.

An atheist, whom I met one day and started talking with, listened politely when we touched upon the faith topic. I testified about Jesus, but received no response. We met several times, but it was like knocking my head against a thick wall. Always this politeness whenever Jesus was mentioned. Never anything more. I was always the one who had to bring up the faith topic, if we were to discuss it.

One day when Christmas was drawing near and I was going to visit her again, I said to the Father: "I have witnessed so many times now, and I feel that I'm not going anywhere fast with this. If You want me to continue, I beg You to make her start talking about faith today."

When we met, our talk was all small talk, but suddenly, without warning, she says to me: "Christmas is right around the corner, and I grew up in a family where we would never read the Bible. Nor have I ever read the Nativity gospel. It's sort of just food and presents at our place. But this year I think I want to suggest for my whole family that we should read the Nativity gospel before we eat dinner. Yes, not only do I want to suggest it, but we certainly shall do so as well."

I was so surprised and happy. This, I had not expected. The words from Isaiah 55:10-11 came to me: *"As the rain and the snow come down from heaven, and do not return to it without watering the earth and making it bud and flourish, so that it yields seed for the sower and bread for the eater, so is my word that goes out from my mouth: It will not return to me empty, but will accomplish what I desire and achieve the purpose for which I sent it."*

When the snow is falling and the days are cold, oh, so cold, it's not always easy to look to the days ahead. Days when the snow is melting and the fields lie black and open after just having been given exactly what they need from the snow, in order for the grain to spring forth in the warmth that bring promises of summer. Then the time has come to look at the snow as a blessing. The word of God can cause questions and opposition – yet it works. The Word works in the depths just as the seed, and gives growth and ripening in due time. For *it shall not return to me empty,* says the Lord.

So I knew that the great sower Himself would step into this home, in which they for the first time would read out loud from the Bible together. And that on Christmas Eve itself!

The Lord Your God Himself Will Walk With You

Many times I've wondered how God could ever choose to call me to preach the gospel about the Lord Jesus Christ. And there are probably many others who have been wondering about the same, as well. A comfort for me has been the words from 1 Corinthians 1:28: *"He chose the lowly things of this world and the despised things – and the things that are not…"* As well as the words from 2 Corinthians 12:9: *"My grace is sufficient for you, for my power is made perfect in weakness."* These have been the core words in comforting me on my journey. He chooses the things that aren't, and His grace is sufficient.

One day, as I was going to an assembly with some other preachers, I was dreading it so much. Many of them had been in this business for many years and were considered celebrities. I didn't know any of them, and I thought that I had nothing to do here in this place. So I prayed to the Father: Perhaps this assembly was not ready-made for me? Then I got the idea that I should check my cell phone to see if there were any new text messages there. And there were.

Marit Kjennstad from Froland by Arendal (a southern town in Norway) had sent me a greeting with the words from Deuteronomy 31:8: *"The Lord himself goes before you and will be with you; he will never leave you nor forsake you. Do not be afraid; do not be discouraged."* I guess I could not have received a clearer answer.

While I was trying to figure out what I was going to wear for the meeting, another text message from the same lady ticked in. She wrote that she had gotten the idea that I had to read verse 6 in Deuteronomy chapter 31. There it said: *"Be strong and courageous. Do not be afraid or terrified because of them, for the Lord your God goes with you; he will never leave you nor forsake you."*

This felt good to receive. So I got myself ready and dashed off. When I was nearing the meeting, I could feel the fear coming back to me. To be both a woman and a preacher among several men is really not always that easy. So I prayed to the Father for another word from Him before I went inside. I recalled the words that had come to me earlier that day, and pondered them. This really was sufficient, but my knees were shaking so badly that they could at least need another word, I thought. Then another text message ticked in. Excited, I fished my cell phone out of my pocket.

It was from Randi Vorhaug in Arendal. She wrote: "I greet you today with this verse from Deuteronomy 31:6: *"Be strong and courageous. Do not be afraid or terrified because of them, for the Lord your God goes with you; he will never leave you nor forsake you."*

Oh, my merciful, good Father! You who look to the sparrow and clothe the lily on the ground, and who tells us that we are worth so much more. Neither of these two ladies had any idea of the situation I was in. Thus, the Father's care felt strong. The Lord was with me – and that was sufficient.

Poetry For the Entire Village

One day a woman called me, asking whether she and some other people could use my poem, "You are never forgotten." These were people from a local congregation who had come up with the idea that they would visit every house in the village with this poem and a flower. Would that be all right? Of course it was. It was more than all right. She told me that they had long been praying for the village and now wanted to reach everyone with a greeting. I thought it was great that someone would use this little poem of mine to bless others. The poem is founded on Isaiah 44:21: *"... I will not forget you."*

Never forgotten
You are never forgotten by God.
He stands beside you now.

Full of mercy in every word.
Let yourself be embraced here on earth.
He defeated death victoriously
because He loves exactly you.
and His words sound tenderly:
you are never forgotten by Me.

Later, the same lady called and reported that all the poems and the flowers had been handed out, and they would continue to pass on this greeting to all newcomers in this village. She also said that when they later had invited the villagers to a meeting in the local chapel, many of the unsaved also joined the meeting.

It can feel lonely to sit and write, or when you go out and preach. Many times I've thought of the word from Ecclesiastes 11:1: *"Ship your grain across the sea; after many days you may receive a return."* Sometimes it feels like I ship my grain across the sea, however, sometimes I catch a glimpse of it returning.

God calls us to bring out the message of our Lord Jesus Christ and the salvation we have in Him. God calls the learned and unlearned. He calls men and women to go out: in neighborhoods, at workplaces, in congregations and further. God calls us to walk together with Him. He calls and equips. One of His promises that He gives us is this: *"Can a mother forget the baby at her breast and have no compassion on the child she has borne? Though she may forget, I will not forget you!"* (Isaiah 49:15)

Be Faithful and Patient

I was in Japan. A lady came over to us while we were attending services in the local church. Her name translated into English meant Mrs. Tortoise-mountain. This was a small but strong lady. She was in her mid-fifties and ran a farm with about fifty milking cows. She rose at around 4 a.m. every Sunday morning to have time to make ready the cow barn before she left for church. Her husband was not a Christian, so she always went alone.

Now she wanted to present us with a gift, which was a message in Vietnamese written by a Vietnamese lady who had stayed in China during World War II. The part of China where she stayed at the time had been occupied by the Japanese. The Japanese arrested her because of her Christian faith and demanded that she fall down and worship the Japanese Emperor as her god. She refused to do so. The Japanese tortured her, but she endured. She placed her hope in Jesus through it all. When she was released, she wrote this message, which has been spread among Christians: BE PATIENT. BE PATIENT ALL INTO ETERNITY. BE HUMBLE.

In Genesis 5, we read about Enoch, who walked faithfully with God. In verse 24 it says: *"Enoch walked faithfully with God; then he was no more, because God took him away."* Nothing more is said about Enoch's walk in the Old Testament. In the New Testament we can read a little more, however not much is told about him here, either. Hebrews 11:5: *"By faith Enoch was taken from this life, so that he did not experience death: 'He could not be found, because God had taken him away.' For before he was taken, he was commended as one who pleased God."* Enoch walked with God, and God delighted in him. To place one's confidence in Jesus' delight means being faithful – and God delights in this. Whether there will be many ordinary days or days full of great challenges, walking in faith means being faithful and obedient to God.

Walk with the Lord every day. Be faithful to Him at home, in your neighborhood, and at work. Be a witness about the Lord Jesus Christ. God calls us to be faithful. Perhaps you'll never see the result of your faithfulness, but walk with Him nevertheless. Turn to Him and be patient. He is the one who shall do the work. *"The one who calls you is faithful, and he will do it"* (1 Thessalonians 5:24).

While I was writing this, an elderly man over ninety years old called from Arendal. He was ill and wanted intercession, but he had learned through a long life with the Lord, that whether God says yes or no, both answers are reflections of His love. He had learned something about patience in his walk with the Lord Jesus, he said. Together we could go to Him who is faithful through it all. To Him who does the work.

The Vietnamese lady had gotten to know Jesus Christ through her everyday walk with Him. The difficult days, too, perhaps especially those days. She had experienced the words in Philippians 4:7: *"And the peace of God, which transcends all understanding, will guard your hearts and your minds in Christ Jesus."*

Let us walk with God and let us turn to Him who does the work. Let us patiently trust the Lord every day and in times to come. For *"...when you say that you do not see him, that your case is before him and you must wait for him."* (Job 35,14)

The Cross of the Three Nails

One day I was asked to join some pastors who were going to the island of Lindisfarne outside the east coast of England.

Lindisfarne is also known as "the Holy Island." As early as 1,400 years ago, Christian monks settled there. They established a brotherhood within the monastery, which sadly was ravaged by Vikings from Norway. Later new monks arrived. Today there are approximately 160 residents on Lindisfarne. What is so extraordinary about this island is that it's only accessible with low tide. The rest of the time it is completely isolated and it's impossible to get there either by foot or by car.

When we arrived in England, one day something unpleasant happened. Such things happen. However, this incident spread consequences that had a painful domino effect. I became discouraged and depressed, and things became difficult. In the morning, meeting with Jesus, I gave it all to Him. I prayed for wisdom in the situation and I also asked for an encouragement from Him that day. I felt strongly that I needed an encouragement after what had happened.

Then I went to the morning mass at 7.30 a.m. in the church. There, an elderly English couple entered and sat down beside me. When the mass had ended, they stopped me as I was going to leave. They told me that what they were about to do now, they had only done once before in their lives. They had been strongly reminded to stop me and give me a silver cross as an encouragement this day. Was I in need of an encouragement, they asked.

This was not just any cross. The cross was made of three nails. During World War II, the Germans had bombed a church in England.

Afterwards, when people searched through the ruins for something worth keeping, they came upon three nails that they strung together with steel wire into the shape of a cross. They called it the Cross of Reconciliation. At the end of the war, some of the local residents traveled to Germany and presented the cross to the authorities there as a sign of their forgiveness, and that they sought reconciliation because of Jesus Christ and what He had done on Calvary.

I had to tell them about my prayer for encouragement and wisdom before the mass. And there and then, in the middle of the church, we remained standing together weeping and thanking Jesus for what He had made us experience and see. We were strangers yet siblings in Christ. In Him, God's only begotten Son, we had sonship. The man said that he usually never heard or felt anything of God's guidance. But on this island it was as though the layer between heaven and earth was so thin due to the many prayers that had been prayed through many centuries. He experienced God's presence so strongly that even he had heard the call to stop me and give me an encouragement.

In my heart, I had forgiven the unpleasant thing that had happened, and now I too walked the road of reconciliation. Also here, the Lord had walked before me, resulting in both reconciliation and blessing.

In the Bible, our walk here on earth is often compared to the walk of the people of Israel in the desert. Despite all Israel's treachery and the multitude of their sins, this truth remained firm throughout the many years of the desert walk: *"By day the Lord went ahead of them in a pillar of cloud to guide them on their way and by night in a pillar of fire to give them light, so that they could travel by day or night. Neither the pillar of cloud by day nor the pillar of fire by night left its place in front of the people."* (Exodus 13.21-22)

The good shepherd always walks ahead to guide us on the right path. Not always the easiest path, but the right one. Be not afraid when you walk alongside Jesus.

He walks before you
The Lord walks before you.
By mercy He is your shield.
He guides you through the night,
and fills you with mercy

when the morning breaks.
He made heaven and earth,
and all that is in them.
And He walks before you.

Tired after a mission

Having had a busy time with many missions, I felt exhausted. Ahead of me lay a trip to the western part of Norway. I felt that I had probably taken too much upon me.

Upon arriving at the place in which I was going to preach, it appeared that those responsible for the meetings were carrying on a feud with one another. Conversations took place and prayers were held, but the conflict wasn't solved. It was a stressful time.

After many meetings and a long journey back home, I was exhausted. I cried out to Jesus in my heart for help – He Himself had indeed been a true human being. Then the phone rang. It was a pastor who had been reminded to call and hear how I was doing. I told him about my trip, the meetings, and the tears in all my tiredness.

He said: "The mission we have been given concerns eternity, and this is part of the reason why we get so involved. When we get physically tired it impacts all areas of life. We were given a cross to carry for Jesus. It's painful and exhausting, and sometimes we have to make a halt. There are times when we can't manage, when we feel that we fail. The great Master Himself could neither manage, so God sent Simon of Cyrene to carry the cross up to Calvary. There are times that we have to tell our friends: I can't take it anymore. The evil one can use this against us as accusations, but the truth is – it's mere tiredness. This was not your conflict, it was theirs. We easily focus on the negative things when instead we should focus on Him who has given us the mission. All works for the good, according to the Word. *"And we know that in all things God works for the good of those who love him, who have been called according to his purpose"* (Rom. 8:28). All it said – even fatigue.

This day, this pastor became my Simon of Cyrene; sent from God to ease my burdens.

Just after this, a text message ticked in on my cell phone from a lady whom I had never met, but who had read some of the books I had written. She had been strongly reminded to send me a greeting: *"Have I not commanded you? Be strong and courageous. Do not be afraid; do not be discouraged, for the Lord your God will be with you wherever you go"* (Joshua 1:9).

She became the second Simon of Cyrene that came this day when I was so tired.

What's so great about being a Christian? Well, Jesus, whom I believe in, weeps. He's not only happy. Twice it is told that Jesus wept: He wept when Lazarus was dead, and He wept over Jerusalem on Palm Sunday. He couldn't force the people into His peace. Our God weeps with us. He enters into our situation. He shared our burdens, sorrows, despair and tiredness. He wants us home, and our mission concerns eternity. The Lord is a God and a Father who is with us in our everyday life. Day by day He is with us.

One of my dear interceders, Ellen Lien, has gone before me home to Jesus. She was born and raised in Telemark, a county southeast in Norway, but as a grown-up she lived in Valle in Setesdal, a valley in a neighboring county. Before she died, she gave me permission to use one of her poems that has meant a lot to me. It's called "Just one day at a time," and was written when her father passed away.

"Just one day at a time"
Just one day at a time. God, help me to understand.
Just one day at a time. That's what I get more from your hand.
Help me, Jesus, to use it right,
and be faithful on the place you have set me in life.

Just one day at a time I was granted from the Lord's hand.
O', let us use it well on our journey to the Heavenly land.
If you see someone tired and despairing as you go along,
stop and tell him that Jesus loves everyone.

Just one day at a time, in sickness and sorrow too.
Rest assured – God is a mighty fortress for you.
You need not carry your burden, Jesus bore it instead.

Just one day at a time. Jesus follows you step by step.

Just one day at a time, when evening draws nigh.
Jesus will stand by my side, even at my last sigh.
You, who are the way and the life. With You we will finally be home.
Indeed, by grace alone, we shall stand in front of His throne. *

Just one day at a time with Jesus, *"Because of the Lord's great love we are not consumed, for his compassions never fail. They are new every morning; great is your faithfulness"* (Lamentations 3:22-23).

* The poem is from Ellen Lien's "Som aaret gaar" ("As the year goes") (*Setesdalsforlaget*, 1997), p. 67, and has been translated into English by Ingunn Oestby.

Clare's Song

It hurts to be rejected, especially when you don't know why. Whoever has experienced this knows something about that pain.

Most people face rejection somewhere in their lives, myself included. Like most women, I immediately took the blame. My thoughts were tumbling around. I went to my Father with this pain, for if there's one thing I've learned, it's that He may have a completely different view on the situation than me. He sees everything. He sees my adversary's heart, what is said and done, both openly and secretly. He also sees my heart and all that is said and done by me. He is my Father and I've learned that I can rely on Him. My prayer was: How do you view this, Father? I'm tired and confused. How shall I go on?

Then Judith Johansen from Farsund (a town in South Norway) called. She wanted to greet me with a few words from her English Bible. She knew nothing about my situation. *"You are altogether beautiful, my love. There is no flaw in you,"* she read from Song of Songs 4:7 (Holy Bible, 1990).

This was so unexpected. Something so completely different from what I had expected. Could I really take this to heart? My head didn't completely manage to follow this turnaround. Thus, I went to the Father one more time and prayed for His affirmation.

Then I received a greeting in the mail containing Clare of Assisi's song. That completely set me free. Clare of Assisi is not as well known as Francis of Assisi, but she was his first female follower. Like Francis, she too came from a very rich family. At 18, she chose to run away from home to become a nun. It was to Francis she recited the conventual vow. Thus the Franciscan convent life for women was founded. They were close and helped each other in advising and guidance throughout life. Their desire was to become more like Jesus.

Bishops and popes alike also held Clare in high esteem, and turned to her several times for advice and help. She was of great significance for the Franciscan movement. Both Francis and Clare chose to live out their faith in poverty and simplicity. Clare died peacefully in 1253 while singing a hymn of praise to God. This was a new song nobody had ever heard before.

And this was the song I received as a greeting. This song set me free. God is good. Hallelujah! He knows our needs and treats us with His fatherly hand of mere grace for the sake of Jesus.

> Clare's last song went like this:
> Walk ahead without fear,
> for you will have a true shield on your journey.
>
> Walk ahead,
> for He who created you
> has blessed you.
>
> He has always taken care of you,
> like a mother takes care of her child,
> and loves you with genuine affection.
>
> I praise you, o' Lord,
> for having created me.

With this song came the peace that transcends all understanding. A silent joy filled my heart, despite what had happened. I praise God, my Father, who shows such grace and care that He sends fellow wanderers with words and a song as a greeting. One word written almost 2,000 years ago, and a song written more than 700 years ago.

The Church Father St. Augustine warned against becoming "lost in oneself." This is what we can become in the presence of hurtfulness and pain. But we can also choose to lift our eyes to the Lord Jesus. He who speaks truth into our hearts. He who gives strength and courage so that we won't go astray or perish. Let us look up to Him, because *"in whom are hidden all the treasures of wisdom and knowledge"* (Colossians 2:3).

Benjamin

It is a great blessing to receive intercession. In Romans 8:34 it is written: *"Christ Jesus who died—more than that, who was raised to life—is at the right hand of God and is also interceding for us."* He who holds the names of Wonderful, Counselor, Mighty God, and Eternal Father, is interceding for us. Sometimes, we are so blessed that we are also given interceders here on earth too – fellow wanderers praying for us.

One day, I was contacted by one of my interceders from Mandal (a city located on the southern coastline of Norway), Bjoerg Berge. She really wanted me to pass on a greeting to Gunhild Eikrem. I told her I would, but first I would like to pray about it.

Then a Bible verse came to me. And soon the greeting was written and passed on to this unfamiliar lady, with prayer that it would bring about great strength and help for her.

A few years later, two women paid me a visit. We had a good time together with Jesus and each other. With the permission from both Bjoerg and Gunhild to mention both their names and what happened, I call on Gunhild herself to recount what had happened:

"After many years as involuntarily childless, I finally became pregnant. It was a joy so incredibly great. Those familiar with the pain related to childlessness, know something about what we had been through. Those not having had to deal with this can probably also sense something about how painful childlessness can be.

"But then we finally got to experience the miracle that I became pregnant. Amazingly I was pregnant with three children. I was very ill the first months, and was in and out of the hospital several times. The anxiety of something going wrong was big. They were so much wanted, these children. We had hoped and longed for this for so long But a pregnancy with three children is a high risk. We were aware of this, and were repeatedly reminded of it by all the hospitalizations.

"At five months pregnant, we were told which sex the children had. There was one boy and two girls. This we didn't tell anybody, not even our parents. It was our little secret. A part of the secret was that the boy's name should be Benjamin, because this name, Benjamin, we had become so certain of.

"On February 23, I received a special card from Rita Aasen. We had never met, but a mutual friend had asked if Rita could send me a few words. Rita prayed about this, and then the words from Deuteronomy 33:12: came to her so strongly. Rather excited, I found my Bible, sat down and started reading. It was then as if Heaven came down. I called for my husband, and while reading to him out loud, my back got the willies by joy and awe. For there it said: *"About Benjamin he said: 'Let the beloved of the Lord rest secure in him, for he shields him all day long, and the one the Lord loves rests between his shoulders.'"*

"In the midst of our anxiety and insecurity, this word came to us. It was very touching and felt good for me in my situation. We got a greater assurance that this should turn out just fine. We became more certain that God really exists – that He sees us and is there for us, and is aware of our situation. The card was written with a 'God-incidence' precisely three months before our children were born.

"We got three healthy children that are now, as I write (Oct. 2008), three and a half years old. Benjamin is the one who has come out of it most strongly, health-wise. We have a very active everyday life with three amazing gifts from God. We are so grateful for these three children that it's hard to even find words that would suffice. They run and play and talk and point – such a delight. Of course it is exhausting too, which is normal, and this is how it should be – but in the midst of it all, the joy is great and deep.

"Benjamin has several times had special thoughts about God that he has told us about. In wonder, we do as Mary did; we guard it in our hearts. And we are continually reminded of the Bible verse Rita sent us: 'About Benjamin he said: *"Let the beloved of the LORD rest secure in him, for he shields him all day long, and the one the LORD loves rests between his shoulders"'* (Deuteronomy 33:12).

"We feel as if we were given a special blessing in which we all can rest. It has been a strong experience, and we just wanted to say: Thank God!"

FORGIVE US OUR DEBTS, AS WE ALSO HAVE FORGIVEN OUR DEBTORS…

Grace isn't Cheap

What do you do when somebody is being manipulative? When somebody lies? What do you do when, in retrospect, you realize you were brought into actions that weren't good? When you as an adult quite simply were fooled. Adam and Eve blamed others even though they were the ones who did the actions specifically. No one forced the fruit into their mouths. They ate it themselves.

The greatest manipulation happens perhaps when we don't take responsibility for our own lives and actions in the midst of what is happening, and as such make ourselves a victim.

To ask questions in retrospect can be helpful. That's what God did in the garden when talking with Adam and Eve after they had eaten the fruit. God made them responsible. He asked them four questions (Genesis 3):

1. "Where are you?"

Ask yourself this question when something goes wrong. Where are you now? Not where the one who fooled you is, but where this brought you.

2. "Who told you that…?"

There will always be some trying to seduce or lead others on the wrong path. The reasons may be many: envy, own personal gain, hatred, revenge, etc. You are the one who decides whom to listen to.

3. "Have you eaten from the tree…?"
God goes to the source. It wasn't the serpent that ate– it was Adam and Eve. Even though they blamed the serpent – God went the way of the truth.

4. "What is this you have done?"
To acknowledge is the way to freedom. It is you who's sitting on the key. Don't blame others, but instead take responsibility for your own life. Then you will be set free.

To be manipulated can make you feel like wanting to hide, just as Adam and Eve did. Isolate yourself. Don't partake like you used to. Live secluded simultaneously as you impose liability on the one who manipulated you, on the serpent in Paradise.

The way to freedom and an upright life goes through the mercy of Christ. You need mercy over your own life – and so does your fellow wanderer. Maybe you want to say that what the serpent did is much worse than what Adam and Eve did. Well… look where that brought them. Outside. They had to leave Paradise. All because of their own actions.

I myself have experienced lies and manipulation, both in Christian contexts and elsewhere. In retrospect, I can say that it was wrong of those who were manipulating, but I have also realized that despite this, I was the one who did the actions they fooled me into. I let it happen, and it cost – in so many ways.

I have also seen that in case I don't forgive and show mercy, I will stay put in the firm grasp of these people. This captivity is full of resentment, and this is preventing the opportunity for change, life, and growth. The way to freedom lies with me, I have the key. The way is called, "Responsibility for my own actions through forgiveness and grace."

Grace is always free, but it is never cheap. To forgive isn't easy on God, either. While sweat turned into blood, Jesus cried out: *"My Father, if it is possible, may this cup be taken from me"* (Matt 26:39). This wasn't an option. Grace cost Jesus everything, but voluntarily He went the way in love.

Forgive us our debts, as we also have forgiven our debtors…

The German theologian, Dietrich Bonhoeffer, who was killed on April 9, 1945 for his battle against Hitler, says this about grace: "the cheap grace is actually the death of the church. The expensive grace cost Christ his life at first, and then a succession that can be heavy to carry is required."

For Bonhoeffer, obedience was also suffering. It might cost to follow Christ, because grace wasn't and still isn't cheap.

Jesus was betrayed by one of His own, but still He presented Judas with the word *"Friend…"* (Matt 26:50). Grace wasn't cheap at that moment.

Jesus was beaten, whipped, scorned, spat at, and crucified together with two rebels, one on each side. And while hanging on the cross, He said: *"Father, forgive them, for they do not know what they are doing"* (Luke 23:34). Grace wasn't cheap in that moment – it was bought at a very high cost.

God has grace for you. He has grace for everything in your life, if only you'll let it in. It is the way to peace. Grace is free for you, but not cheap. That's why Jesus hung on the cross. You are bought at a high price. So is your fellow wanderer. To forgive those who hurt us is the key to personal peace.

In Romans chapter 12, Paul says:
- *Be devoted to one another in love.*
- *Honor one another.*
- *Never be lacking in zeal, but keep your spiritual fervor, serving the Lord.*
- *Practice hospitality.*
- *Bless those who persecute you.*
- *Do not be conceited.*
- *Do not repay anyone evil for evil.*
- *If it is possible, as far as it depends on you, live at peace with everyone.*
- *Revenge….is mine to avenge…says the Lord.*
- *If your enemy is hungry, feed him.*
- *If he is thirsty, give him something to drink.*
- *In doing this, you will heap burning coals on his head.*
- *Do not be overcome by evil, but overcome evil with good.*

It concerns your soul. The Lord wants you all the way home. Consequently, Jesus fought on the Calvary cross and won victory over the forces of death. Over all evil. Over all sin. Jesus wouldn't be defeated, not once. As such, you shouldn't either. Give room for the highly expensive grace.

When David confessed his sins, manipulation and adultery with Bathsheba and the murder of her husband, Uriah, he wrote in Psalm 51:12: *"Restore to me the joy of your salvation and grant me a willing spirit, to sustain me."* For it concerned his life, his soul. David learned this essential life lesson of which he writes about in Psalm 54:6: *"I will sacrifice a freewill offering to you; I will praise your name, Lord, for it is good."*

Live in God's expensively bought grace for you and your life, and for your fellow wanderers' lives. Put your trust in the Lord, your God. *"For the Lord will be at your side and will keep your foot from being snared"* (Proverbs 3:26).

God's amazing gift: Forgiveness

It has been told that a guest in a monastery asked an old monk after a few days about what they really were doing there. According to the Father of Spiritual Communal Monastic Life, Pachomius, the monk answered: "We rise and fall, and rise and fall, and rise and fall, and rise again."

When reading this, my mind went to the little poem I had written a few years earlier. A niece about to have her confirmation had been given an assignment – to read a poem on her day of confirmation. She wanted me to write one to her. I prayed for a short and easily understood text, yet still with some depth that she could carry with her the rest of her life. This was what she was given:

One and a thousand times
If you fall
and fall
and fall again
indeed, if you fall one thousand times

Forgive us our debts, as we also have forgiven our debtors...

and the others
must carry you
and guide you forward
then it is
that you rise in the light of the cross
for the one thousandth time
that is the most important
of everything
you will ever do
of everything
you do in your life.

The old monk said that they rose and fell, and rose again. This is the same thing we do outside the walls of monastery. It's called – walking with God. In Micah 7:8, it says: *"Do not gloat over me, my enemy! Though I have fallen, I will rise. Though I sit in darkness, the Lord will be my light."* The Lord, He who gives us compensation, again and again, through forgiveness and mercy.

A while ago, I spoke at a women's conference one weekend on Solstrand near Vigeland, not far from Mandal (a city in South Norway).

Here I got to know Judith Johannesen, who was an officer of the Salvation Army. She was a major, and Africa had become her workstation. She had been a missionary there for several years, yes, in fact, her whole working life. We had several good conversations.

One day, she told me about an incident that had left deep marks. I asked whether she would like to write it down for me, and if I may use it for this book. She did.

Every human being is a worthy of a whole book. Perhaps even many books. Life meets us with good and with bad. And we all have something to learn from each other.

What Judith told me happened in Rhodesia in 1978, known as Zimbabwe from 1980 and onwards. Judith had some good friends and missionary colleagues working at a missionary school there. The school was located outside a city east in the country, close to the border of Mozambique. This area was starting to get more and more unsafe and dangerous as guerilla groups were constantly crossing the border. They killed several people in the area, and left immense destruction behind.

The principal of this missionary school thus found it necessary to find new buildings inside the city border for their work, and in doing so, increase the safety for the missionaries and their families. As principal, he had busy days and had to travel to England, among other things. On his way there, he stopped in the closest city to look for buildings they could use when he would return. From there he continued his trip to England.

Thus, the principal wasn't on the missionary station that night when the horrible thing happened. A group of armed men had managed to cross the border from Mozambique and made their way to the missionary station and the school area. Here they gathered all the missionaries from their homes, and their children, sixteen people altogether, and brought them to an open, spacious place. All adults, children, and an infant were killed before they left the area again.

The shock and pain that the principal experienced upon his return was indescribable, and he had to take on the painful and difficult task of burying his friends, colleagues and their children.

Afterwards, he traveled to England to inform the missionaries' families of how it all had happened.

A few years later, the principal from this little missionary school became a pastor for a congregation in Harare.

His congregation grew in number, and continually more people were attending his church services. One Sunday, a few people came, who apparently were new to this church. The pastor greeted and welcomed them to the congregation.

After the service, the newcomers recounted how God had met them, how they had become Christians. They told that a few years earlier, they had been in a guerrilla group that one night and had crossed the border from Mozambique to Rhodesia. There they had come to a missionary station with some foreign missionaries and their children. They had killed every one of them.

But all the missionaries had said—even upon facing death—that they forgave them. Before the missionaries were killed, they had prayed out loud for the murderers and told them that they had to ask God for forgiveness. This had a strong impact on the murderers.

Forgive us our debts, as we also have forgiven our debtors…

The guerilla force had violence and death as its strength, but the missionaries had something even stronger. As such, a part of the guerilla group went on and crossed the border to Botswana. There they found a congregation and a few who could bring them to Jesus. Later on, they went to Bible school to be trained in the basics about the faith in the Lord Jesus Christ.

A few years later, when Rhodesia had become Zimbabwe, these new Christians traveled to Harare in hopes of finding work and a new congregation they could join there.

And so they had come to this congregation, where they had hoped they could start attending, they said. The pastor sat quietly and listened to their story. He who earlier had been the principal of this very missionary school, and who had lost all his loved colleagues, friends and their children, was now sitting there struggling with his own feelings, at the same time that he knew he had forgiven this.

He had been the principal in the very school they were telling about. That it was he who had found his friends dead and who had to bury them all. But he had, like his friends, the missionaries, also forgiven the murderers. He knew that this God-given gift, forgiveness, would help them now as well, to become a part of his congregation.

Forgiveness is a gift for everyday use, in destruction, in degradation, and in the events that we can't make our minds fathom and take. Only God can give wisdom and power in the Lord Jesus Christ to live in daily forgiveness. Forgiveness is a gift to raise again, but forgiveness is never cheap. Never. Jesus knows this, He who is the conqueror of all sin and death. God makes miracles happen, and forgiveness is like a miracle in our lives.

The missionaries sowed a seed the day they were killed. It can seem pointless to sow such a small seed. It's placed in black dirt, and we never see it again. But God makes miracles in the dark, hidden for our eyes to see. Let us not sow to please the flesh, because this only reaps destruction. Let us sow in the Spirit. Paul writes in Galatians 6:8: *"Whoever sows to please their flesh, from the flesh will reap destruction; whoever sows to please the Spirit, from the Spirit will reap eternal life."*

Turn to Him, and help will be given you. In Psalm 121, verses 1 and 2, the psalmist testifies: *"I lift up my eyes to the mountains — where does my help come from? My help comes from the Lord, the Maker of heaven and earth."* He had experienced that help is given by turning to the Lord. As Paul said in Romans 5:20: *"...where sin increased, grace increased all the more."*

Do you love me?

Peter had walked together with Jesus for three years, but when difficult situations arose, he failed. After this, Jesus asked: *"Simon son of John, do you love me?"* (John 21:15-91) Peter failed, but he had chosen to confess and settle this account. Then Peter was confronted with another a new choice, and this time Jesus made it possible for him to find the right way from there onwards. He asked the same questions which was the most important for the walk ahead: *Simon... do you love me?*

To betray others hurts. To be betrayed also hurts. I've experienced both. The times I have failed, and then looked for reconciliation and settlement, the result has been renewed fellowship. But the road hasn't been easy. It has taken time. Today too, Jesus asks: Do you love?

Once when I was betrayed and the person concerned had confessed and accounted for it, no further walk together was made. It was painful. After a while, I took courage and tried to get in touch, but was rejected. Later I tried again, but was rejected again. Then I went to the Father again with all of it. That evening, I received a greeting from Farsund (a town in South Norway) with the words from Jeremiah 16:19: *"O Lord, my strength, and my fortress, and my refuge in the day of affliction"* (KJV). Then a text message ticked in on my cell phone from the Vaagsbygd suburb in Kristiansand (another city in South Norway) with the words from Exodus 3:7: *"The Lord said, 'I have indeed seen the misery of my people in Egypt...and I am concerned about their suffering.'"* This was a good comforter even though there was no solution to the issue. I had been seen by my heavenly Father, and in the midst of pain He sent His word to me through people who knew nothing about my situation.

Forgive us our debts, as we also have forgiven our debtors...

Paul writes in Romans 12:2: *"...be transformed by the renewing of your mind. Then you will be able to test and approve what God's will is—his good, pleasing and perfect will."* No one possesses such deep psychological insight as God. When somebody betrays and makes right again, and they choose to walk the way of love together, then you and your neighbor are both healed. This can only happen through love, something Jesus showed. This is why Peter was asked: "Do you love me?" Here the whole secret lies: Have you love? In Corinthians 13:8, Paul says: *"Love never fails."*

It's instinctive for a human to tend to the justice of the self. Some also choose the role of the victim, not wanting to take responsibility for their actions. They're not willing to admit that what they say and do, or what they don't say and do, affect the situation and the way ahead. The choice is ours today. Are you willing to love? It doesn't help that your morality and façade are in good shape. The question always will be: Do you love me?

Thus, let us pray that the words in 2 Thessalonians 3:5 must become the reality of our lives: *"And the Lord direct your hearts into the love of God, and into the patient waiting for Christ"* (KJV).

For it is written in 1 John 2:6: *"Whoever claims to live in him must live as Jesus did."*

There are times when violence and crazy actions cause us to separate, but through it all the verse says: *"Above all else, guard your heart, for everything you do flows from it"* (Proverbs 4:23). Jesus speaks truth into our everyday lives, in the midst of strife, arguing, divorce, hatred, rejection, selfishness, and jealousy. He knows that we are failing, and that we will be betrayed. Thus, He came to earth. He chose the way of the cross, to speak of what value every one of us has. He chose the nails to illustrate what our betrayal has cost Him. He chose obedience to God so that we should have the opportunity of forgiveness. He chose love to show us the way He calls us to follow Him daily.

In 1 John 3:10-11, John writes: *"This is how we know who the children of God are and who the children of the devil are: Anyone who does not do what is right is not God's child, nor is anyone who does not love their brother and sister. For this is the message you heard from the beginning: We should love one another."*

Peter had the choice: Do you love me? Every day, we face the same choice. We can choose justice to the self, the role of the victim, or the way of love. We can shape our own and our neighbor's next life when we choose. Jesus calls us to forgiveness and confrontation. He calls us to reconciliation. It's not always successful, but we shall always, as far as we are able to, work for it to happen – even though we're the ones who will be betrayed. For forgiveness is first and foremost a gift to yourself.

After betrayal and confrontation, Jesus asked this question: Do you love me? For the confrontation isn't the end. The way goes on.

Let us give room for love. Let us walk together with Jesus, because: *"He heals the brokenhearted and binds up their wounds."* (Psalm 147,3) And in Isaiah 41:13, He says: *"For I am the Lord your God who takes hold of your right hand and says to you, Do not fear; I will help you."*

I WILL INSTRUCT YOU AND
TEACH YOU IN THE WAY
YOU SHOULD GO...

The Biggest Crown

When I was called to preach the gospel about the Lord Jesus Christ, the Savior, both my husband and I decided to face this calling together. We prayed about the missions and the walk, and it was a strength to stand together in this. But after a while, I started having some problems. Because whenever I was out and spoke, I received all the attention and praise, and often a flower thrown in, but no one but me ever gave my husband praise and attention. And to me, he was just as much into this as I was. Without us standing side by side, I could not have answered to this calling.

I brought this up with my husband, but for him this was completely unproblematic. Maybe I should've just left it at that, but I so wholeheartedly wanted him to be seen in the intercession service that he was responsible for. He was so important to me, because without intercession I will never stand on a speaker's platform.

When I went to the Father with this, I was so reminded to go to the bookshelf and pick one specific book. I opened it by chance, and there my gaze fell on an article about an officer of the Salvation Army. His name was Smith, and he had traveled and preached the gospel in many countries and continents. He had been in many awakenings. One day, when he was home taking a nap after dinner, he experienced that an angel came to him in his dreams. The angel asked whether he would like to take a little trip to heaven. Yes, he would. When they arrived, Smith saw several magnificent crowns, but one of them was greater and more magnificent than others. He thought that perhaps that one was his. Indeed, he had been in many awakenings and traveled so much and preached for many years. Then the angel asked whether he wanted to know who was to receive the greatest crown. Oh, yes, indeed he would, Smith said in phony modesty. "This," the angel said, "will be given to she who was on her knees in prayer at home when you were out preaching."

This was an incredibly good speech to me. What a Father we have. Hallelujah, I say. He is wise and good. This little article set me free, completely. All was good. Kaare should get what he deserved. Indeed, God is good. In Jeremiah 32, verses 17 and 19, it is written: *"Ah, Sovereign Lord, you have made the heavens and the earth by your great power and outstretched arm. Nothing is too hard for you. Great are your purposes and mighty are your deeds. Your eyes are open to the ways of all mankind; you reward each person according to their conduct and as their deeds deserve."*

An Extra Flight

I was in Stavanger (a town on the west coast of Norway) and preached. The flight was purchased, but it wasn't possible to get a direct flight to Kristiansand on the way back. I had to go through Oslo. Thus I went late that night and waited in the big departure hall in Oslo Airport, Gardermoen, on the last plane home. I started praying to the Father. "Why do You want me all the way here to Oslo? It is a huge detour. If there is something You want with this, I'm here." Suddenly, while I was walking and praying, I heard somebody calling my name. It was a married couple I had met earlier one day when I was preaching in their chapel in Arendal (a city in the South Norway). Now they were waiting on a plane to Haugesund, a city located on the West coast of Norway. Among other things, they were going to visit a friend who was very ill.

While sitting there and talking together, I was reminded to send a little poem with them to the sick lady. They would gladly bring it with them, they said. Then we went our separate ways.

A while after this, I received a phone call from the sick woman they were going to visit. She thanked me for the poem and told me: When they came, she had just been lying and reading one of my poetry books. In it was a special poem she had become very fond of. This she told them, and then read out loud. Then they told her that they had met me on their way there, and I had sent with them a poem as a greeting – this they had not read yet. When she opened it, it turned out that's the poem I sent was exactly the same poem she had just read out loud for her guests!

He walks ahead of you
The Lord walks ahead of you.
By mercy He is your shield.
He guides you through the night,
and fills you with mercy
when the morning comes.
He created heaven and earth,
the sea and all that it contains.
And He walks ahead of you.

However we are feeling, we can trust that the Lord sees us and shows us fatherly care. This woman was never healed, but she got strength for the days to come. She got strength from Him who sees every one of us. He who sent me to Oslo, so that she would see His care for her. In Isaiah 41:10, He says: *"So do not fear, for I am with you; do not be dismayed, for I am your God. I will strengthen you and help you; I will uphold you with my righteous right hand."*

Further, in verses 17 to 21, the Lord says:
"The poor and needy search for water, but there is none; their tongues are parched with thirst. But I the Lord will answer them; I, the God of Israel, will not forsake them. I will make rivers flow on barren heights, and springs within the valleys. I will turn the desert into pools of water, and the parched ground into springs. I will put in the desert the cedar and the acacia, the myrtle and the olive. I will set junipers in the wasteland, the fir and the cypress together, so that people may see and know, may consider and understand, that the hand of the Lord has done this, that the Holy One of Israel has created it. 'Present your case,' says the Lord. 'Set forth your arguments,' says Jacob's King."

Three Things Within an Hour

I was asked to preach at a women's meeting on Vegaardshei, a municipality in Aust-Agder county, Norway. After praying about it, I accepted, and we agreed that I should come back to them with a theme when the meeting was drawing closer. It was a few months in advance.

Sometimes when I'm out preaching, I bring with me a team that are interceders, some decorate, some play to the worship music, and so forth. About three weeks before this meeting should take place, I received a text message on my cell phone from the lady who was to come with me and decorate—Arnhild Aasland from Finsland, a city in South Norway. She wrote: have you come closer to a decision for a theme for the sermon at Vegaardshei?" I had not, so I sat down and started to pray about it. At once I struck me that the theme should be "God-given talents." Everything we have are gifts from the Lord, and it is up to us to use these gifts to honor God. Here, every one of us has a responsibility and a choice for our own life. I texted the theme back to her: "God-given talents," and she replied straight away that she had been reminded repeatedly to decorate with a lot of wrapped-up gifts. They were supposed to be a visible symbol for God's gifts and talents for us.

Right after that, the contact I had at Vegaardshei called me and wondered whether I had come up with a theme for the night. Then I could tell her what had just happened. Many months had passed since the phone call about this mission, and then, on this day, everything fell into place, within one hour. A coincidence? No. God-incidence, if you ask me.

In Isaiah 45:11, it says: *"This is what the Lord says—the Holy One of Israel, and its Maker: Concerning things to come, do you question me about my children, or give me orders about the work of my hands?"*

"Enlarge the place of your tent"

Isaiah 54:2
I was called and asked whether I would volunteer to do unpaid work in God's Kingdom. I was pleased for the enquiry, but how did

I will instruct you and teach you in the way you should go...

---

the Lord view this? Would He want me to do such work? Would He want me to dispose my time like this? I had to pray for help to see what He wanted me to see.

The same day a text message ticked in on my cell phone with a greeting from a woman. She wrote that it was suitable, and greeted me with verse 20 from 1 Chronicles 28: *"Be strong and courageous, and do the work. Do not be afraid or discouraged, for the Lord God, my God, is with you. He will not fail you or forsake you until all the work for the service of the temple of the Lord is finished."*

Three days later, I was going to preach at a meeting. During the meeting, a woman came forward. She had been strongly reminded to read from Isaiah 54:2-3: *"Enlarge the place of your tent, stretch your tent curtains wide, do not hold back; lengthen your cords, strengthen your stakes. For you will spread out to the right and to the left; your descendants will dispossess nations and settle in their desolate cities."*

This spoke so directly to me that I decided to accept the unpaid work.

Former bishop Georg Hille, now bishop emeritus, who also had a bishop father (both actually staying at Hamar–a town in East Norway inland) once told Vaart Land (a Christian Norwegian newspaper) in an interview about how he experiences God's guidance: "God speaks to me through His word, His will comes to me so vividly that I can't escape it." The other method through events that just make everything so prepared so that God's plan is unarguable. The last method is to use people that are perceived to be sent from God.

For instance, a friend of mine called me one night in 1970, when I was a pastor in Lom, a municipality in Oppland county, Norway.

"He asked whether I had applied for the director job in the church council. I hadn't. Then he told me to send a telegram that very night."

But Hille didn't send any telegram that night, because he didn't understand why he was supposed to join the church council. However, the day after this, during his devotional time, God came to him so strongly in the Bible texts he was reading, that he no longer could doubt that this was the road God wanted him to take. He said: "It happens sometimes, that you can almost hear the voice while reading. I just had to close the book and send that telegram."

He continued: "Had I not read that chapter at that very moment, I wouldn't have wound up in the Synod, and surely not as bishop either. And that is almost my whole life."

Hille chose to follow God's guidance. So shall we ordinary walkers be allowed to do. For God doesn't have favorites, nor does He differentiate between people. In 2 Chronicles 14:11, Asa puts it this way: *"Lord, there is no one like you to help the powerless against the mighty."*

Undaunted, we all can turn to God to be guided to the next step on the road we shall walk. *"For we are God's handiwork, created in Christ Jesus to do good works, which God prepared in advance for us to do"* (Ephesians 2:10).

Our help rests with the Lord, our God and Father. That doesn't mean that salvation comes in good deeds. No, for it also says: *"We... know that a person is not justified by the works of the law, but by faith in Jesus Christ"* (Galatians 2:15-16).

Our help
Our help
is in the name of the Lord.
He who created heaven and earth.
He is the One
who clears the way
so that not even fools shall walk astray.
He is the One
who gives grace,
so that we will have truth in our hearts.
He is the One who says:
If you stay with Me,
always I will be with you.

A Willing Heart

For many years now, there have been arranged several joint meetings in Kristiansand Cathedral. In relation to this, several of the meetings have been broadcasted. A few years back, I was asked by

I will instruct you and teach you in the way you should go...

the joint meeting committee whether I could take responsibility for two hours of live coverage after the broadcasts. After prayer, I felt at peace to accept this offer. For the last five years I have participated, and several great guests have been in studio with strong testimonies about what Jesus means in their daily lives – it was a gift to be a part of this.

There is a lot to be done, prior to inviting the guests to come. The first thing is interceders. I will never stand on a platform nor in a studio without interceders. So, every year there are five ladies who specifically pray for this work. That gives me strength. It ensures that it will be easier to find those who will be our guests.

One of the guests I was once reminded to ask was a wonderful lady who herself works with radio, Margrethe Tveit. She is the general manager of *Radio Philadephia* in Kristiansand. "I've been waiting for this," she said, "because a while ago I felt that God told me to share my testimony with you someday."

This was great news! I asked her to write it down, so that I could use this in my book. She did, and from here I'll let Margrethe Tveit herself do the narration:

"Once, Rita, when we sat and talked together, God spoke to me. Not with an audible voice, but I knew it was God who told me to share my testimony in a context where you were involved, and that you would ask me about my story. Since I don't have a whole lot of experience in talking to people, I was a little scared that you would ask me in a situation where many were gathered. To me it was a lot easier to talk about Jesus and who He is, rather than sharing my personal testimony. It's easy because He is so wonderful and so good. To share my testimony about my life, my faith, and my way, I found a little difficult. I work in radio broadcasting and like to talk and work with words, so that in itself isn't an issue. To talk in the presence of an audience is a little different than sitting in a studio and 'talk with the mic.' In an audience there are so many eyes, and to see the people you're talking to is a completely different feeling.

"Although this sounded a little scary, I said yes to God: If the occasion arrives, and Rita asks, I will say yes, No matter what situation I'm facing, for you have prepared me for it. Whether it is one person or a thousand that will be listening doesn't matter as long as it is You who have asked me to do it.

"I was so sure of this being God speaking to me, that I sat down and wrote some points, dates, and occurrences, so that I would have everything ready, and all the details would be correct. I formulated it almost as a little speech, and folded the papers together and put them in my purse.

"There they lay for several months. I can't remember how long, but it was probably close to half a year. Every time I went through my purse to clean it, my common sense told me to throw away the papers as I met you so many times during this period of time, and not once did you ask me to share my testimony! But the quiet voice that I recognize as the Holy Spirit, continuously told me that you were going to ask, so the papers still lay in my purse. They became more and more worn-out, but I never removed them.

"When you were going to lead the radio programs in relation to the joint meetings in Kristiansand, the question came. And all the time I had thought it would never happen. I didn't have to stand on a platform and dread that all the people would watch me, because I was invited to a studio where I had my daily job and felt a hundred percent at home.

"There you interviewed me about my walk with Jesus. I felt safe in the situation, and I got to share my testimony with the population of Kristiansand and on 'home ground.' I got to talk more about Jesus than about myself. I could read through the tattered papers in my purse and put them away, because all of my nerves were completely gone.

"It's fantastic how God guides, even in the small everyday life situations. It's safe to walk with Jesus, because He always walks in front and guides us."

Paul writes in 1 Corinthians 1:4: *"I always thank my God for you because of his grace given you in Christ Jesus."*

It's wonderful when somebody testifies about the Lord Jesus and His work at Calvary. It's wonderful when somebody testifies about Him and his or her walk with Him in everyday life. Because He will walk with us every day, all of us who come to Him. He has said that He will be with us, always. That doesn't mean that all days will be good. It will be a diversity of days, but the Lord Jesus has promised to be with us all those different days.

When we walk with Jesus, our normal state is Psalm 37:4: *"Commit your way to the Lord; trust in him and he will do this..."* All He asks for is a willing heart.

HE KNOWS OUR NEEDS...

The Flour Jar and the Oil Jug

We had lived at an ancestral farm of my husband's for twenty-two years, when one of our sons wanted to take over. We agreed that us "old people" would need a year to find a home. We prayed to God about where He wanted us. Because of my husband's driving distance to work, we were interested in looking at houses on the distance between Spangereid and Kristiansand (South Norway). When we prayed for a new home, we also included a wish for five different things in our new home. Among other things, a workroom for my pottery, and an office.

For weeks and months we searched, and searched. None of the houses we had looked at had a workroom or an office. When almost a year had gone by, we saw a house on the Internet that had a workroom and an office, and that was on sale. Bids had been made, and when we called, we were told that it was going to be sold the next day. Thus, if we were interested, we had to come straight away and off we went. The house was everything we had prayed for. And the workroom and the office were wall to wall. Excellent.

But the cost was too high. What then do you do, when you pray and receive an answer, but still think the cost is too high? Then you pray again. We felt good about placing an offer and the next day we received a call that the house was ours! It all happened so fast, I felt completely shaky.

When I sat down to give thanks, a sudden fear came over me. What if we couldn't make this work financially? We believed that we would make it, yet my thoughts ran off just the same. I placed it all before the Father. While I was in prayer, a text message ticked in on my cell phone. It was from a lady in Kristiansand. She knew nothing about our house purchase, but she wrote that she had been strongly reminded to give me a word from 1 Kings 17:14: "For this is what the Lord, the God of Israel, says: *'The jar of flour will not be used up and the jug of oil will not run dry'...*" She hoped it fit. Truly, it did, and indeed it arrived in the nick of time.

When we moved, we saw that it was as if the house was built for us. All our furniture fit, down to the inches. And the jar of flour and the jug of oil have not run dry. The Lord kept His word. He can be trusted. In Psalm 23, David writes: *"The Lord is my shepherd, I lack nothing."*

This trustworthiness from the Lord is something we have experienced on the farm for the twenty-three years we lived there. Even though I didn't see it at the moment, I see it now.

David trusted the Lord, just as he writes in Psalm 25:2: *"In you, Lord my God, I put my trust."* So will I.

Pay from the Lord

When the service of preaching the Gospel about the Lord Jesus Christ began, it also became clear that this would be a tentmaking service. The kind that Paul the apostle had, and many after him. Paul preached the Gospel without taking pay for it, but he sewed tents that he sold to earn money for a living (Acts 18:2-4). This is where the word "tentmaker" becomes a symbol of evangelization service, where pay comes from another occupation. When my tentmaking service began, I was always certain that this should last till I was about halfway in my life. From there I should start taking pay for the service. Sometimes I thought about what should happen in the middle of my life, as this felt so real to me. And now I'm there, and we've moved to a new place because one of our sons wanted to take over the ancestral farm.

Several times had I been encouraged by other preachers to take pay for my service. They had always used the word from 1 Tim 5:18 as their argument: *"The worker deserves his wages."* About this they're right, yet not before now have I been able to feel at peace for

He knows our needs...

doing so. Being a woman and a freelancer is not always easy in all situations. Whenever there is collection during a meeting, much of the money goes to pay the permanently employed in an organization. This is right in God's kingdom. But those who work as freelancers would also need milk and bread on the table. Sometimes when I'm asked to preach, and I mention pay, some refuse. Then I would still preach, of course, because that's what's most important, it's my calling. And I trust in the Lord that He will provide for me just as He has promised.

Once when I had preached at four meetings in four different places, a little in rapid succession, I received a no for both pay and gas money for the first meeting. I didn't get anything for the second nor the third either, but I put everything in the Lord's hands.

When I came to the fourth meeting, and they wanted to settle an account afterwards, I was told that the congregation had been given such a peace and agreed give me a certain amount of money. It turned out that the sum was exactly the equivalent pay for four meetings. I had never experienced anything like this ever before, and asked whether they could afford it. They told me that they had joyfully agreed to do this – this was mine. The gas expenses were also covered. I had to smile, yes, laugh a little inside about what the Lord had done. He paid me pay for all meetings.

On my way home from this meeting, I received a text message on my cell phone from a woman in Kristiansand who knew nothing about this. She just wanted to greet me with: *"The jar of flour will not be used up and the jug of oil will not run dry."* The words are taken from 1 Kings 17:1-16, where the story goes about Elijah the prophet, the famine, and the widow in Sarepta. In verse 16 it says: *"For the jar of flour was not used up and the jug of oil did not run dry, in keeping with the word of the LORD..."* A song of praise to the Lord and His doing was sung.

The words from Matthew 6:33 have also been very important to me. They show me where to begin the day with the Lord and His word, but also in seeking Him first of all in everything that comes in many a weekday. *"But seek first his kingdom and his righteousness, and all these things will be given to you as well."*

This doesn't mean that we get whatever we ask for. Not at all. But the Lord has opened a new way for us. And this is how we are raised, to thank Him for what He gives us and be certain that this too is enough.

Angel and Salary

I was asked if I could preach at a meeting, but there would be no pay for the mission. I said yes to the request, and left the question of payment in the Lord's hands. When the day of my departure arrived, I felt very tired for different reasons. My thoughts had tumbled, wondering if I should have said no. I just felt as if I couldn't do it. So there I was, tired and exhausted. Then the phone rang. It was a lady who said that she had been reminded to hand me two verses from Isaiah 41:9-10. She hoped it would be useful. And there it said:

"I took you from the ends of the earth, from its farthest corners I called you. I said, 'You are my servant'; I have chosen you and have not rejected you. So do not fear, for I am with you; do not be dismayed, for I am your God. I will strengthen you and help you; I will uphold you with my righteous right hand."

God is good. I chose to look up to Him. I chose to trust Him. Then I left with the message I felt He had given me. It felt great to be a part of the fellowship of those who came to the meeting. I had brought candles with me that they could light and put next to the cross. Many came forward and lit their candle. At the very ending, a lady came forward and gave her life anew to Christ. It was great to see her beam with happiness. I thanked the Father for what He had done. And this gave me renewed strength in my ministry.

The day after my return home, I received a package in the mail. It was a greeting from Ingjeborg Elinor Rysstad from Rysstad in the Setesdal. She said that she wanted to contribute sowing in the Kingdom of God. Thus she sent me a beautiful angel of glass and a sum of money. The sum equaled the payment I was supposed to have received as a salary. That was how the Lord, my God and Father, took care of this matter.

In Isaiah 57:10, the Lord declares: *"You wearied yourself by such going about, but you would not say, 'It is hopeless.' You found renewal of your strength, and so you did not faint."* Yes, truly, His Word is indeed the truth. It is also written: *"...he will satisfy your needs in a sun-scorched land..."* (Isaiah 58:11).

Laser Printer

We own a laptop. It's connected to the Internet, but we didn't have a printer for it. Consequently, this caused difficulties whenever I received a report by mail, for instance, as I couldn't print it out.

Thus I went to look for a printer. Several people had recommended a laser printer, since it was supposed to be cheap to run. However, when I checked the prices, I thought them to be too expensive. I decided to wait with this purchase.

I was told in the store that they would soon receive a laser printer that would be cheaper than the ones I had been looking at. They could write down my name and number, and notify me as soon as it had arrived. I thought about this in the days that followed. Should I, or should I not purchase this? I wasn't sure. I prayed.

Then one day, a lady called me. She said that she had been reminded during prayer that I had something that I was pondering whether I should buy. And whatever I was supposed to buy, she would pay for. She said she felt that this had come vividly before her from the Lord, and now she wanted to ask me whether I was pondering about something. Perhaps a book or a bag? Whatever it was, I could just go ahead and buy it. She would pay for it. Was she right in what she had understood in her prayer, that I was thinking of buying something?

I confirmed that she was right, but it was neither a book nor a bag. It was a laser printer. "Go and buy it, and send me the bill," she said. I tried to explain how much it cost, but it didn't matter. Just go and buy it, she said.

Half an hour later, the store called and told me that the laser printer had now arrived. It was ready if I wanted to buy it. I felt a little shaky. Could I do this? Accept a whole printer? Then all of a sudden a text message ticked in on my cell phone – from the same lady who had called earlier. She wrote: There is no price restriction for the printer. You need to get one that will meet your needs. Just go ahead and buy it.

So I got myself a printer. I went to pick up the one I had thought about buying, and that Jesus had reminded her to pay for.

In 2 Corinthians 9:6-7, Paul writes: *"Remember this: Whoever sows sparingly will also reap sparingly, and whoever sows generously will also reap generously. Each of you should give what you have decided in your heart to give, not reluctantly or under compulsion, for God loves a cheerful giver."* May the Lord bless her abundantly, so that she will reap as abundantly as she sowed.

And in verse 8, Paul continues: *"And God is able to bless you abundantly, so that in all things at all times, having all that you need, you will abound in every good work."*

Printing Cards in Faith

Walking in faith is not always so easy. There are times when we feel that we can move mountains with our amount of faith, and there are times when we have hardly any faith at all. It is important to put our faith in the Lord, and not in our amount of faith. For it is not our faith that can, nor shall do the work. It is solely the Lord Jesus who shall do it. Thus our eyes must be fixed on Him alone. Then the faith in Him will grow and receive the right perspective. To sit down by His feet and listen to Him and to what He wants to guide you towards is necessary so that you can receive the help you need to walk step by step with Him in faith, in your everyday life.

A friend of mine, Olaug Aa, makes watercolor paintings. One day she asked me whether I could make cards out of her painting together with my poetry. That, I would love to do. I prayed to the Father whether this was His way for us. We felt at peace about this. The cards were made, and I brought them along to meetings when I was out preaching. This was also a way of spreading the gospel. Then, one year, well ahead of Christmas, she called and asked whether we should make more cards. By now she had several new motif, among them a Christmas motif. Again I prayed. What would the Father like? This time, however, we got no peace to start making these cards, and thus we put the matter aside.

He knows our needs…

Christmas came and left, but the cards and the texts just lay waiting. Printing cards is also a financial matter. Actually, I was glad that I didn't receive any all-clear signal to start the printing process, as the economy didn't permit it at that time.

But then in January, the all-clear to start printing came. Olaug experienced a serene, inner conviction that just kept growing stronger every day. So did I. However, I only had NOK 300 (about USD 50) on the account meant for such purposes. What I should I do? Again, I prayed, and again this strange peace for printing the cards came about.

To walk in faith is literally just that – walking without seeing. So the cards were ordered. The day before they were finished, I received a phone call from the United States. A lady called and told me that she had read my book, *In God's hand,* that had been published in the U.S., and she had now been strongly reminded to give me a gift. Further, she told me that she had some stock in a bank. This bank had now been closed down, and thus she had been given quite a sum of money during this settlement. Her husband had asked what she would use this money for, and she had replied that she wanted to give it to people that the Lord had reminded her of. That was all right by him, and so she started giving – and now she had been reminded of me. And it turned out that the same day that the bill for the cards arrived, a letter from the bank about the money from the United States had been transferred to the account. All I had to do was pay.

When the people of Israel were facing the Red Sea with the Egyptian army behind them, Moses raised his staff, trusting God, and the Lord parted the sea. Furthermore, in Exodus 14:22, it is written: *"And the Israelites went through the sea on dry ground, with a wall of water on their right and on their left."*

Why is it that we find it easier to believe this, than the fact that God can lend us help in our everyday life? In Hebrews 13:8, it says: *"Jesus Christ is the same yesterday and today and forever."*

New Flatware

When we married, we had bought flatware, and over the years we used this diligently. But one day I thought that it started to have a taste of metal to it. By then we had used it for over twenty years. I didn't like the idea that the children and we adults might get certain metals in our systems that weren't healthy for us. I prayed to the Father about this. This prayer was about a new set of flatware. At that time we lived at a farm in Sogne in South Norway, and I welcomed groups of people who wanted to look at the pottery I was making. Normally they would also like me to have a devotional or read some of my poems. It was a great opportunity to testify about Jesus. Many of those who ordered pottery or arranged for a meeting with me were searching for a goal and a purpose in life.

One day, a large group from Kvinesdal came. They looked at the pottery, and I held a devotional afterwards. Then followed a wonderful meal with food they had brought along with them. Afterwards, some of them wanted to see my workroom. Just as they were heading out the door, one of the ladies approached me. She had struck me as one of the most quiet and modest ones. Now she whispered to me that she had been reminded to give me this – she placed her briefcase next to my feet and ran outside. I had many goodbyes to make, so when I went to thank her, she had already left.

I opened the briefcase and found a set of flatware for twelve persons! I was so happy. The praise and gratefulness went to my heavenly Father for His goodness and generosity. When my husband came home, I showed him what we had been given. He looked at the suitcase and said: "There's more!" Then he removed what to me had appeared to be the bottom of the briefcase and uncovered another layer of different tools: ladles for sauces, cake forks, cake servers, etc.

It was such generosity from the Lord that I can still feel how overwhelmed I was. Again, I thanked the Father for what He had done in the midst of our everyday walk with Him. The flatware was replaced, and the new adopted – and how wonderful it was to sit down at the table with this set of cutlery! To see what the Lord had done brought joy, hope and faith.

I managed to track down the lady who had given us the flatware and told her about my prayer regarding a new set of cutlery, and I thanked her for her obedience. Feel free to write about this, she said, just leave my name out of it. In great joy and gratitude we both thanked God for the work He had done in our lives. In Matthew 7:11, it is written about our heavenly Father: *"If you, then, though you are evil, know how to give good gifts to your children, how much more will your Father in heaven give good gifts to those who ask him!"*

Closed Doors

Trials may come when we walk with the Lord. In a family with two little children, both parents lost their jobs. The despair was high and the prayers many. I too prayed for them. The father in that family applied for a job which he had a great possibility of achieving, but the answer was no. The mother didn't succeed in getting the kind of job that they needed.

I continued praying for them. Then one day while I was at *Holmely Retreat Center* on Bryggja, located on the western coast of Norway, and preached, I met the fabric designer, Eli Hegrestad. She had made several beautiful pictures, some with biblical motifs. Some of them weren't downright biblical, but they had great symbolic meanings.

One of the pictures was made as a house. It had a closed door, but above the door was a large, open window facing an astounding, beautiful landscape. On the roof it was written: "When one door closes, a window is opened." The priest for KRIK (CHRISC–Christian Sports Contact) once said that "when the doors close, don't give up, but find a window."

I immediately felt that God wanted me to give this picture to the married couple that was struggling so hard with finding new jobs, as an encouragement and a help on the way. I asked whether it was for sale. Eli Hegrestad said that many had wanted to buy it, but she hadn't wanted to sell it. However, if I wanted it, I could buy it. The price was NOK 1,500 (about USD 257).

I told her that I wanted to give it away to a family that was experiencing closed doors. She then told me that she wanted to reduce the price to NOK 1,000 (about USD 171), should I wish to buy it. The deal was that I should get back to her the same evening.

While I was walking away from that place, I started praying. "Am I thinking right about this? Is this Your will, Father? If it is, then I pray that You help me with these NOK 1,000. And another thing: I pray that a text message will be on my cell phone from this family when I come home to my room. And let it be a sign that this is Your will and way in this matter." I did what Gideon did, and laid out a wool fleece (see Judges 6:36-40).

While I was wandering on, praying, a lady who had been at the meetings came up. She stopped me and told me that on the occasion of my 50th birthday she wanted to give me a 1,000 NOK in advance as a part of the birthday present. And there I was, with the money I had prayed for, all of a sudden placed in my hand.

When I came back to my room, I was excited whether a text message was waiting from this family. And it was.

I went back that evening with a certainty in my heart and the money in my pocket, that this was the way to go. The Father had given me both signs that I had prayed for. But when I wanted to pay for the picture, Eli Hegrestad said that she too had prayed, and now she wanted to give this picture as a gift. And that was it. The picture was sent, and I got to keep my birthday gift. It happened just like David testified about in Psalm 23:1: *"The Lord is my shepherd, I lack nothing."*

I told the family that was in this difficult situation that a picture would come to them in the mail, and that this picture was a gift from the artist herself, Eli Hegrestad and me. I didn't mention the symbolic meaning – that was to be a surprise.

The day the picture came, the family had a visit by a priest. He wanted to console them in their difficult situation. He said that sometimes God closes a door just so that He can open a new one. Just then they recalled the picture. They opened it and saw this closed door and the window in the picture. It was a powerful experience.

God's caring was there in the midst of the difficulties. Not too long after this, both of them found jobs, but through the difficulty they had experienced that God was with them. In Deuteronomy 8:2, it is written: *"Remember how the Lord your God led you all the way..."*

The Bible tells us that it is important to bear in mind how God leads, and how He is always on the way that He leads us. Joshua was also reminded about this. In Joshua 4:1-7, we can read about when the Israelites had crossed the Jordan. God brought them over with dry feet in the midst of a time of flooding. God is very specific in the situation and tells Joshua that he should let twelve men each bring a rock with them from the riverbed. These rocks were supposed to be a reminder of how God had delivered His people and helped them through the difficulties. The rocks were supposed to give the Israelites an opportunity to tell their children about God's reliability, so that future families would also learn *"the way the Lord...your God has led you..."*

The picture that this family received can be this memorial stone. And, God receives His glory among us.

Do You Always Receive Answers to Prayers?

Sometimes I get this question: Do you always receive answers to prayers, huh? I felt like asking a question in return: What is an answer to prayer? An answer to prayer can be a lot of different things. It can be a clear, an obvious, and a definite answer to direct, specific prayers. But it can also be an answer that is harder to gauge, like when we ask for someone to be preserved by Jesus. An answer to prayer can also be that God says no. Or it can be that God doesn't think it's the proper time yet to give you whatever you're praying for. Perhaps many forget what they were praying for, and once the answer presents itself, there will be no glory and thanks to God for what He gave. Answers to prayers are so many-sided.

I have participated in a lot of courses over the years. My prayer has been that God would lead me to what is ready-made for my walk, and that He must provide for it all financially as well, He who has called me to serve in His vineyard. As a spiritual counselor, I have found great joy from courses at *Institutt for Sjelesorg at Modum Bad* – an institute for spiritual counseling at Modum, Norway. For all the courses I have attended, the course fee has come at the right time, in a strange way – in the Lord's way. Now, some might say that in today's Norway you can afford to pay. Indeed, they're right, we do have the opportunity to save money. However, as a freelance preacher, I don't have an employer who supports me financially and sends me on different missions, thus I seek the Lord who has called me to minister, and ask for guidance and help.

The home-staying son in Luke 15 said: *"...Yet you never gave me..."* (v.29). The answer that his father gave him, has often been spoken to me: *"My son...you are always with me, and everything I have is yours"* (v.31).

Everything I have is yours. However, this doesn't mean that God is a slot machine of fortune. Yet we can carry everything to Him. He is our Father.

Several times over the years, I have prayed for means for courses or further training, without it falling into place and me not falling into rest regarding this. I will mention one particular occasion: We were two female preachers who took a course at Modum together. There we were informed that it was possible to take pastoral clinical education through them in Kristiansand, my hometown. I had prayed several times for this to happen, and now everything fell into place, I thought. Yet, no matter how I prayed, I felt a deep unease – and hence I didn't apply. However, the lady I had studied together with did apply. She got accepted, and finished a year later.

Similar things have happened to me several times. I have, as far as I can judge, had the opportunity and the desire, but have been stopped. Whether I have chosen the right path regarding this, the Lord only knows, however in retrospect it has become evident that it would've been difficult had I started attending these courses. Thus, I have settled down with this: if the Lord is my shepherd, I lack nothing (Psalm 23:1). These things were not part of my walk, and so they are also answers to prayer. The Lord sees it all. And I only know in part, and see piece by piece (1 Corinthians 13:12).

But, after years of prayer for additional training in spiritual counseling, and With continuous no's from my heavenly Father, one evening I came across an advertisement in the Norwegian Christian newspaper, *Vaart Land*. It was about a course in further training in spiritual counseling through the MF Norwegian School of Theology, the institute for spiritual counseling at Modum, and the Church of Sweden. It was as if I heard a resounding yes in my heart from the Father when I prayed for permission. After all these years of no's, there suddenly came a yes. For a moment I was a little taken aback. I was more prepared for another no.

He knows our needs...

The following day, I called and was told that I could apply, however the course was primarily meant for priests and deacons, so such appliers would be given top priority. And there was another thing: Since I wasn't employed and connected with a bishops office where I could apply for financial support regarding the fee, I would receive a bill privately of NOK 28,000 (about USD 4,620) should I be accepted. If I would still be interested in applying, then I was welcome to do so.

This phone call took place at 10 a.m., and at 11 a.m. my sister Nina called. I told her about the situation, and she said: "We need to pray for means, because if this is the Lord's way, He will provide for you." Right there and then, we prayed a simple prayer to the Father about His will and way in all this, and specifically for NOK 28,000.

At 12 p.m., a lady called asking whether she could come for a visit as she had something she wanted to give me. When she came, she handed me NOK 28,000. She knew nothing regarding what we had been praying for.

As I write this, I have applied and been accepted at this study program. I haven't started yet, but I look forward to it with joy in prayer and hope that I will make it. For without Jesus, I can do nothing.

The verses from Psalm 23 have meant much to me in my walk with Jesus. When I pray and wait for an answer, these have often been a resting place for me. If the matter is put in the Lord's hands, I'm certain that there can be no safer place. I know in part and haven't got the whole overview, but I choose to rely on the Lord.

This is a choice I have to make every day. Especially on days and times when He is invisibly present. David writes: *"He guides me along the right paths for his name's sake"* (Psalm 23:3).

He guides and leads for His name's sake. Then the whole foundation for it all is in Him. This is called a walk of grace.

FEAR NOT, FOR I AM WITH YOU …

Butterflies and Wandering

The road we wander can be compared to the process a butterfly must go through. In the catacombs where some of the first people who knew Christ are buried, there are butterflies carved in the walls. They tell of a secret of transformation, hope and resurrection. We can find butterflies forged into iron crosses on old Norwegian tombs. In John 11:25-26, the Lord Jesus Christ says: *"I am the resurrection and the life. The one who believes in me will live, even though they die; and whoever lives by believing in me will never die."*

God allows miracles to happen all the time. Miracles that we can't even see. By using the butterfly, God teaches us about life. Have you ever seen a butterfly break out from a chrysalis? That is an awful struggle, almost like a death struggle. Maybe this, only the butterfly would know. But one thing's for sure – it is an exhausting struggle. The butterfly must force itself out of the shell from its old life, the life it once lived.

It's the only life it knew of. And although it was a hard one, it was safe all the same. The caterpillar spins its own chrysalis from the body's own silk filament, and falls asleep. Unaware of what's going to happen, its life is lived in a dark, narrow cave, where there is no opening nor way to be seen. The body turns grayer and grayer. It's all a mystery, which nobody can explain, but the truth is that a recreation takes place in there. Those who have tried to penetrate into the hidden life receive no answer. In there, in the hibernation the transformation takes place, and the caterpillar loses itself. But one day it knows that the time has come for it to break itself out of the chrysalis. To become something new, it has to break out of the shell. The chrysalis has been spun over time by filaments from the caterpillar itself. Now it yearns for freedom, but it's held captive. Some of the filaments are harder to break than others. The struggle for freedom can be both frightening and painful. When you watch a butterfly fighting and struggling, you may feel tempted to stoop down and help it. It would've been so easy to just tear some filaments, just a few. It would've made the struggle so much easier, and the butterfly would never have to know. But this must never be done. Doing this would've destroyed it. It would die. Butterflies have a center in their bellies full of fluid for filling the veins in the butterfly wings. It's the pressure generated from the struggle, and the pressure to break free from the prison of the chrysalis, which itself created, that force the fluid out from the center in the belly and into the veins on the wings. Without the fluid, the winds could never fold out completely, and the butterfly would never be able to fly. But once broken free, it can lift its wings and soar toward the sky in a new form, a form it could never have dreamed of. It comes with a message of hope, freedom, transformation and resurrection to all those wanting to see and hear.

Don't be afraid if you're facing a struggle. Turn to God. He has a plan for every human being. In an African song, it says:

If a grain of sand can turn into a pearl, and a caterpillar turn into a butterfly, love can change the world.

You can, just like this butterfly, become something you never even dared to hope for. You can join in and bring the message of hope to others. For His love brings healing, transformation, and new life. In John 17:26, Jesus says: *"...the love you have for me may be in them and that I myself may be in them."*

Be not afraid! The Lord Himself is with you. He loves you dearly. He says: *"Forget the former things; do not dwell on the past. See, I am doing a new thing! Now it springs up..."* (Isaiah 43:18-19).

Light For the Walk Home -

One day in the beginning of August, I received a call from a married couple, Oddfrid and Arne Winterstoe in Farsund, a town in the southern part of Norway. Arne had been diagnosed with cancer and they wanted intercession. That I promised them. When I prayed for them in the days that followed, I was reminded of the words from Isaiah 41:10: *"So do not fear, for I am with you; do not be dismayed, for I am your God. I will strengthen you and help you; I will uphold you with my righteous right hand."*

I called and greeted him with words from Isaiah, and he thanked me warmly. Not long after, he called me again. He told me that not long after I had called and reminded him of the words from Isaiah 41:10, he had received a bouquet of flowers from "Broderkretsen paa Havet" (a Christian association for Norwegian sailors) where he was a member. They greeted with the same verses. And the same evening, he had again been reminded of the same words from Isaiah by some friends of his. Three times had he received this greeting that very day. This moved him strongly, for in just a few days he would start on his chemotherapy.

We had a conversation about Him who never leaves nor forsakes us. And who illuminates the journey all the way home while He says: *So do not fear, for I am with you.*

An old story is told about two Native Americans who watched the building of a lighthouse by the American coastline. The day the lighthouse was ready with lights, foghorn, and bell, that day everything was wrapped up in fog.

One of the Native Americans said to the other: Light is shining, bell is ringing, horn is sounding, yet the fog is just as thick as before.

There was something they hadn't gotten ahold of, something essential. Something that was hidden from them. A secret.

The lighthouse had not put an end to the darkness and the fog, but those who wanted to find the way home now had the opportunity through the darkness and the fog. They had a light to follow. A light to show them the right way home.

Jesus says about Himself in John 8:12: *"I am the light of the world. Whoever follows me will never walk in darkness, but will have the light of life."*

The secret is Jesus. He is "the Way" home. Have you accepted Jesus as your Lord and Savior? You have everything you need, for whoever accepts Him will be saved. In Romans 10:13 it is written: *"Everyone who calls on the name of the Lord will be saved."*

In Christ you have peace with God, and in Christ you will be watched over as a child of God. For He is mighty to protect you. Here on earth, Jesus is with us, and when we're called home to Him, we're with Him. In December the same year, Arne went home to Jesus. But not alone. For as David writes in Psalm 23:4: *"Even though I walk through the darkest valley, I will fear no evil, for you are with me..."* You're never alone when you have put your faith in the Lords Jesus and the salvation we have through Him. You're never alone, for He will walk with you all the way. Yes, even through death. He will never leave you nor forsake you. He will lead you to Him who wipes away tears and makes everything new. *"He will wipe every tear from their eyes. There will be no more death or mourning or crying or pain, for the old order of things has passed away"* (Revelation 21:4).

No One Will Make You Afraid

We were some women traveling together on a mission trip. At the place we were staying overnight, something scary happened in one of the neighboring rooms, and we gathered to pray over what had happened. But not everyone could settle down easily that night. On the following day, we were asked to return later that winter. Again we gathered to pray. One of the women prayed for a sign showing us whether we should return, and this she received. Thus we promised to come, though there was still some uncertainty concerning what had just happened.

When I returned home that evening, I placed the whole matter before the Father. Not long after, a text message ticked in from Marit Viki Barstad in Valle. She had been reminded of a word from Leviticus 26:6: *"I will grant peace in the land, and you will lie down and no one will make you afraid."* It was like a balm and with joy I could pass it on to the others I had been together with on the trip.

And what He said happened. Some time later, when we visited the same place, there was nothing that scared us. The Lord granted peace for the whole place. He let us walk upright in the ministry, and we could rest without anything scaring us. In Leviticus 26:13, the Lord says: *"I am the Lord your God, who brought you out of Egypt so that you would no longer be slaves to the Egyptians; I broke the bars of your yoke and enabled you to walk with heads held high."*

I Fear Not For the Night

This title is the beginning of a song written by Haik Hovsepian Mehr from Iran. I've never met him nor talked to him. Still, he is one of those who have meant much for me as a Christian through what he has written and done. The first time I heard of him was right before the start of a broadcast, which I was going to have in "Soegne church radio." He had been to Kristiansand in 1985 and recorded a CD with his own songs at Gimlekollen Media center, to be more exact *Lynor*.

I had gotten hold of this CD. The lyrics touched me. The songs were partly sung by himself in his own mother tongue, and partly in Norwegian by Magne Fremmerlid and Nils Harald Soedal. Haik had made the texts and the melodies himself. He took the Iranian version with him back to Iran for evangelization purposes.

Two of the songs I played more often than the rest. Parts of one of them go like this:

When one day my journey is ended,
my soul stands there perfectly free.
When I stand there by the gates of Heaven,
all sin and all grief will fade away.

Till the day I behold my Savior,
I will love and serve Him here.
I will watch and wait in prayer,
till I meet my groom, God's son.

Haik was born in Teheran in 1945. He was a shoeshine in his early days. He was saved at an early age, and after a while he also became a pastor. Later he became the leader of all the Protestant Christian churches in Iran. A cousin of his, Pastor Saro Khachiki, put it this way: "From a human perspective no one could imagine that a shoeshine boy from a poor family could one day become the head of the nation's churches and be leading others." And Pastor Vartan A. Vanesian described him this way: "He was as peaceable as a lamb, but as a leader he was unshakeable."

When one of Haik's Christian brothers, who had been imprisoned for ten years for his faith, was sentenced to death, Haik, putting his own life at risk, went out internationally and fought for him. And won.

On January 12, 1994, Mehdi Dibaj was released only days before his death sentence was to be carried out. Three days after this, Haik disappeared. No one knew his whereabouts. The government informed his family eleven days later that Haik was dead. He was killed by multiple stabs. He was found in a roadside ditch. He became a martyr.

Haik once said in a sermon: "In God's eyes there isn't a great distance between this world and the one to come. It's like moving from one room to the other. For the one who lives with this conviction, death is no great matter."

When I heard about Haik's death, I was strongly moved. I knew that he had had his life threatened even before he visited Kristiansand and recorded the CD. Now it had happened. He was a brave and humble man, highly loved and respected. He often said that he was ready to die for his faith in the Lord Jesus Christ.

A memorial service was held in Westminister Abbey in London, where present Norwegian Bishop Kvarme spoke.

I wanted to share this, as I'm convinced that we are shaped by the people and the incidents that we encounter. Haik chose to stand for what he believed in. This has been a part of showing me the way of my walk also. I wish to testify for the Lord Jesus Christ in my own way. Haik has inspired me to do so.

The other song that I have often played on Sogne church radio, and that Haik wrote, is this:

God, I fear not for the night,
for You have lit the stars
They stand and beckon me home to You,
when my work day has come to an end.

They remind me of Your faithfulness,
of every promise that You gave.

They remind of Your mercy,
of the bottomless sea of grace.

I see a star rise in the east,
it shines brightly on my way.
God, I fear not for the night,
You Yourself are my light.

At the memorial service in Westminster Abbey, Jerry Parsely also spoke, and together with him I say: "We say good night, Haik, and see you again tomorrow."

Loved and Unique

A letter came in the mail from a lady. She wrote: "You are unique. Greetings with Zephaniah 3:17: *"The Lord your God is with you, the Mighty Warrior who saves. He will take great delight in you; in his love he will no longer rebuke you, but will rejoice over you with singing."*

Just after I received this, I experienced being manipulated and betrayed. It didn't feel at all as if I was loved or unique, or that the Lord rejoiced in me.

When someone betrays you, it hurts. It could be family members, friends, someone in the congregation, at work, or people you trust. And the feeling of not being valuable or loved can soon get its grip on you. Now I had experienced betrayal. I tried to make use of rational thinking and reason in the situation to place the problem where it belonged. But this didn't help. The experience of not being loved or valuable held me firmly. I prayed to my Heavenly Father for help. but nothing happened, as far as I could see. A while later, I met a fellow wanderer in the Lord, and we had a good long conversation. We shared from our lives with one another under the promise of secrecy. Slowly I started to put what had happened into words.

Then, just as we were in the middle of sitting and talking about this, a text message ticked in. It was from a lady who knew nothing about my situation. She wrote: "God loves you. You're the most beautiful that exists. He says: No one is like you. You're unique. You're my child. Your value is immense. This I showed you on Calvary where I bought your freedom. I wish you too could see it this way. I love you. You are unique."

Suddenly I recalled the card that I had received with the same text – that I was unique. It was as if heaven opened, in me and around me. It was as if time stood still for a moment of peaceful timelessness. Something fundamental entered my consciousness and my heart. I was loved.

The betrayal and the hurtful experiences became something that had happened in the periphery. The Lord had answered before it happened, and He was with me through it all. He replied afterwards as well, with the same message: You're unique and loved.

On Calvary, Jesus showed us the truth about our lives. He showed us the greatest love that has ever been given us. We're all loved and unique. In Christ we are all granted forgiveness and mercy for all that we bring forth into the light from the cross at Calvary.

Sometimes we get injuries and wounds. Sometimes they're deep and it seems impossible to forgive. Let us turn to God, He who went the road to Calvary for you and me, yes for all human beings. Let there be room for His love. He loves you with eternal love. Let Him speak truth into your life. For *"… our struggle is not against flesh and blood, but against the rulers, against the authorities, against the powers of this dark world and against the spiritual forces of evil in the heavenly realms"* (Ephesians 6:12).

The Danish bishop Georg S. Geil once wrote this:

Before me is a road that I don't know,
a path, which leads somewhere that I don't know.
I know nothing of what tomorrow brings,
whether the day brings battles or peace.
But this I know: My life is in God's hands, and God is eternal love.

You're loved and unique. In Jeremiah 31:3, the Lord says: *"I have loved you with an everlasting love; I have drawn you with unfailing kindness."*

Fear not, for I am with you ...

All Your Children

John Hardan from the broadcast series, "Vindu mot livet" (Window towards life) once said: "I don't know how many promises there are in the Bible, but I have read somewhere that there should be about 36,000. That means a hundred new promises for every day in a year. Or one new promise every day through a hundred years."

I don't know whether this is correct, but when God gives you a promise in your life or in your family, then cling to what the Lord then gives. In the fullness of time it will come true if it is from the Lord.

Children are a blessing. Many joys, but also trials, come along with children. The childhood and adolescence of children can vary greatly, even among siblings, and there comes a time when they have to make choices for their own lives. As parents, we borrow the children for a while, we do not own them. We shall love them and guide them, but they have their own lives to live.

When one of our children got caught up in something, which made us anxious, we prayed to God. We prayed together as parents, and did what we could from the conditions we had, but we saw no change.

Then one day I was praying together with a sister in the Lord. We placed the whole matter before the Lord and asked for help. This mother's heart was fearful. Just as we were praying about this that worried me so much, the phone rang. It was from Johanna Skogli from Loen in Stryn, a mountainous region in central Norway. She wanted to thank me for a greeting she had received from me. She said: "I told God just before I called you that I would love to have a word to give to Rita as well. Do you have one for her? And immediately a word stood clearly before me from Isaiah 54:13: *'All your children will be taught by the LORD, and great will be their peace.'* I hope this fits."

It fit right into the situation. I wept for joy. Just as we were praying for our child, this answer came. It couldn't have been better, I thought.

Two days later a text message ticked in, from a lady who also didn't know about our situation. She wrote that she just wanted to greet me with Isaiah 54:13: *"All your children will be taught by the Lord, and great will be their peace."*

It was the best a mother's heart could have received. God often confirms by using two or three witnesses. So I kept these promises in my heart as precious gems. This happened a while ago. Now everything is fine with the boy. The Lord was with us. He didn't let us walk alone. He was with us in every step. He who loves my children so much that He gave his one and only Son, Jesus Christ, so that they could live with Him, in Him I will put my trust. Also regarding the children. It is a choice. The words from Exodus 16:12 stood before me where the Lord promises the children of Israel to grant them what they need on their way to the Promised Land. The Lord spoke and said: *"At twilight you shall eat meat, and in the morning you shall have your fill of bread."*

And what the Lord said happened. During the whole walk in the desert, the people had their promises fulfilled. During the whole walk in the desert.

Sow in Weakness

I had been through times that had been demanding in many ways. Now I was facing a tour of preaching to a different part of the country. Not much strength was left. The day before my departure, I sought God first in the morning with Bible and prayer, as I usually do. I placed my situation before Him. Since He is Lord, I have to seek Him first. I sat reading the Word, and suddenly it was if a sentence in the text, 1 Corinthians 15:43, spoke directly to me: *"...it is sown in weakness, it is raised in power."* I had to read the words over and over again. *It is sown in weakness, it is raised in power.* This gave new encouragement. I didn't gain new strength right there and then, but I received new encouragement to go ahead together with the Lord. He was going to sow His word, even though I was weak. He would make what had been sown rise in His power. Then I felt safe. His strength is enough. He alone receives all honor. All was well.

The same morning, a lady who knew nothing about my tour of preaching called. She said she had been reminded to tell me: *"It will be sown into blessing."* She hoped it fit the situation. It was a blessing and a confirmation, I thought.

Paul writes in 2 Corinthians 12 about the thorn in the flesh. Three times he pleaded to be spared from his torments, but nothing happened. In verse 10 he says: *"That is why, for Christ's sake, I delight in weaknesses, in insults, in hardships, in persecutions, in difficulties. For when I am weak, then I am strong."*

God doesn't show favoritism. He is the same God and the same heavenly Father you and I turn to. In Him I put my faith, He who alone does the work. He who says in His word: *"It is sown in weakness, it is raised in power."*

The Lord Will Fight For You

When many people are together, each has a life story. We all travel with different baggage, and that will influence the fellowship. This is true at a working place, in the congregation, in the family, among friends, and so forth.

Once when we were many Christians gathered together, I noticed that one person who was a fellow worker constantly avoided me. After a while this became obvious to the others as well. She didn't greet me, nor talked to me, and left when I arrived, even though I tried in many ways that we could meet. I was confused. I couldn't think of anything unsettled between us. But as Christians, we should live in the light, according to the scripture, so I placed this before the Father and prayed for wisdom.

Maybe it was something that I had said or done that I was unaware of, which the other person held against me. The Holy Spirit convinces us about sin, so I prayed that I had to see if there was anything I had to settle. But nothing came to me.

When nothing seemed to improve between us, I thought I had to ask whether we could have a talk and to bring the matter into light. Again I sat down in prayer to the Father. Then, unexpectedly a text message ticked in on my cell phone from a lady. She wanted to greet me with: "The Lord will fight for you!"

Amazing Father! The sender knew nothing about what I had been sitting and praying about. What a word! The Lord Himself will fight for me and sort out the matter. Thus I was anxious to see how this encounter with the lady would turn out when I was to meet her the following day. Would it be another rejection?

When we met, I was completely astonished. The lady smiled and warmly greeted me and talked with me several times. It was a total turnabout of behavior. What had happened between her and the Father is something only they know. But I was very happy about the outcome. From then on, the ministry in which we were in became a whole lot easier I gave thanks and praise to the Father for both the word and the help He gave me in my time of need. The Lord says in Isaiah 45:11: *"This is what the Lord says — the Holy One of Israel, and its Maker: Concerning things to come, do you question me about my children, or give me orders about the work of my hands?"*

Jesus is with you in the Furnace

A lady called me and told met that her sister had been diagnosed with cancer. Would I pray for her? I'd love to.

Some time later she called me again, this time announcing that her sister had gone home to Jesus. But the two sisters had experienced something together, which this lady now wished to tell me. She bought my book, *In God's Hand,* and she had mailed it to the cancer hospital where her sister was.

That very day that the book arrived in the mail, her sister had been lying and praying to God whether He could send her an encouragement, and when the book came in the door, she felt as if it was an answer to her prayer. She had been very happy and grateful.

We prayed for healing for her, and we didn't get it. She prayed for an encouragement, and got it. The Lord moves in mysterious ways.

It can be tough for our faith to be tested when we face distress and sickness. *But poor is the one who doesn't have any Father to turn to in all his times of trouble. Rich is the one who can say Abba Father, and leave the day and the night to Him.*

When Daniel's three friends were thrown into the furnace, they were not alone. Another one was there with them. There were four of them in the furnace. In Daniel 3:25, we can read that: *"He said, 'Look!*

I see four men walking around in the fire, unbound and unharmed, and the fourth looks like a son of the gods.'"

The Lord is the one who will never leave you when you put your faith in Him. Whatever you're going through, whether it's heading homeward, or towards more days here on earth, He will never leave you. You're not alone.

I myself have been in such a furnace once. We were in Spain, and in the (Norwegian) seamen's church in Torrevieja we heard about a local Christian potter. In his family he was one in the line of many potters. We traveled and visited him, and it was indeed a powerful experience. It was even more fun for me since I have a master certificate as a potter.

The potter had many ovens in his workshop. Among others was an oven built after the same principle as the one we read about in the book of Daniel. Outside the oven hung an illustrated poster with a drawing of a furnace and the account of Daniel's friends and the furnace.

The oven that this potter had was large. We tried, and easily fit five people inside it. After this I thought it was easier to visualize the four characters as described in the furnace in the book of Daniel. Daniel's three friends, who found themselves facing a hard test they couldn't control – and with them, the Lord Jesus Himself. They were not alone.

As Christians, we may be facing great trials and incidents in life. Sometimes we make it through, other times we make it home.

In Psalm 63:3, David testifies: *"Because your love is better than life."* And in Psalm 37:28: *"For the Lord loves the just and will not forsake his faithful ones."*

Let us then pray like Moses did: *"Teach us to number our days, that we may gain a heart of wisdom."* Psalm 90:12

In the Valley of Death

I was called to a lady who was suffering from terminal cancer. Both she and her family wished me to anoint and pray for her. The extraordinary thing was that we had attended school together. None of us knows what tomorrow brings. Sickness may present an opportunity to prepare oneself more than a sudden accident, but one can never be completely prepared for death. Death can sometimes be experienced as something final for the ones left behind, but for the believer, death is not final, because we have a hope in heaven, in the Lord Jesus Christ. He has gone before us, and He says to each one of us in John 14:1-3:

"Do not let your hearts be troubled. You believe in God; believe also in me. My Father's house has many rooms; if that were not so, would I have told you that I am going there to prepare a place for you? And if I go and prepare a place for you, I will come back and take you to be with me that you also may be where I am."

Jesus has prepared a room for each one who wishes to come to Him. If you at your last second in life want to come, you will be saved for eternity. All is made ready by Jesus. It's only for you to accept it.

Before traveling to see my friend from school and her family, I prayed to the Lord for some words on my journey. Words that could speak to all of them, whatever the outcome would be. Then this came to me:

I'll never leave you
Your shield
is with God.
With Him
who never leaves you.
With Him
who never lets you go.
With Him
who gives you to drink
from deep water wells
in the middle of the desert.
He strengthens your soul.
He alone says:
Don't be afraid.
I'm with you.
I carry you step by step.
Never will I leave you;
never will I forsake you,
because I love you with all my heart.

I'm here for you, now
and forever more,
My beloved,
beloved child.

This was brought along to this lady and every member of her family. The lady was anointed and prayed for, and they put all their faith in Jesus.

Not long after, she went home to Him who never leaves us nor forsakes us, to Him who guards us through the valley of death. He who has gone before and prepared a room exactly for her. To Him who says in John 14:1-2; *"Do not let your hearts be troubled. You believe in God; believe also in me. My Father's house has many rooms."*

I hope that you too who read this can also find comfort and hope from these words by Jesus and this little poem. This lady went home to Jesus. Her family was left to continue their everyday life, but Jesus is just as much present with them as He is with her who went before them. He has given us many promises in the Bible. One of them is found in Hebrews 13:5: *"Never will I leave you; never will I forsake you."* This promise lasts for time and eternity for you if you wish to receive Him, and thus be granted a room made ready for you as well.

A Disciple's Tongue

When we pray to our Father for guidance to walk rightly, and difficulties occur, we can become unsure. I had prayed for help regarding a choice of path. A clear guidance came to me, and the road lay open in front of me. For a short distance it went well, but then difficulties arose. I was confused and prayed for advice and guidance. Then I read in my morning devotional from Exodus 17:1: *"The whole Israelite community set out from the Desert of Sin, traveling from place to place as the Lord commanded. They camped at Rephidim, but there was no water for the people to drink."*

The people went on the Lord's command. A command is a powerful word. They had been walking rightly before the Lord, and still difficulties arose – they lacked water. It was absolutely crucial to have water to survive in the desert. This granted me peace that I had wandered rightly even though difficulties had occurred along the way. I had to pray for help and wisdom for what I was facing.

I had met people who considered my words unusable. It's indeed my words that make up my instrument in books, on the pulpit, and in mass media. What was I to do? Was there a lesson to be taught here? I was completely stuck, indeed tongue-tied. Again I cried out to the Father.

Then I received a greeting from theologian, Oeyvind Benestad, in Kristiansand. He just wanted to give the words from Isaiah 50:4-10, and they spoke directly into the situation I was facing. My tears were running in gratitude to the Father as I read: *"The Sovereign Lord has given me a well-instructed tongue, to know the word that sustains the weary. He wakens me morning by morning, wakens my ear to listen like one being instructed."*

The peace that transcends all understanding filled my heart. I couldn't have been given clearer words than these. A disciple's tongue. The tongue is the tool for the words, and indeed my tongue was given to comfort tired souls, the Lord said. I want to listen to what the Lord says along the way. To Him I want to listen.

In Deuteronomy 33:3, Moses says towards the end of his life: *"Surely it is you who love the people; all the holy ones are in your hand. At your feet they all bow down, and from you receive instruction…"*

Then a greeting came from Anne-Lise Dybdahl Ostensvik in Tysvaer.

She wrote: "In the midst of trials and difficulties, our heavenly Father longs to pour out His help. God wishes to bless you. God wishes to use you. God wishes to give you strength. God wishes to protect you. This is our great God.." Again I thanked the Father for His confirmation at the right time. We are never alone.

Asaf testifies in Psalm 78:52-54: *"But he brought his people out like a flock; he led them like sheep through the wilderness. He guided them safely, so they were unafraid; but the sea engulfed their enemies. And so he brought them to the border of his holy land, to the hill country his right hand had taken."*

The Lord hasn't changed. He led his people safely through the desert in times gone by. He will lead us today as well.

"THE LORD SUSTAINS THEM ON THEIR SICKBED AND RESTORES THEM FROM THEIR BED OF ILLNESS"
Psalm 41:3

Wherever You Are, There Jesus Will Be

Once I felt very ill and was admitted to the hospital in acute condition. After some time, I was moved into a double room where a lady in her fifties was already lying. When we were left alone, she came over to my bed and wanted to greet me. I was still feeling so ill that all I said to her was: "Can we talk tomorrow?" Then I fell asleep.

When I woke up the following morning, she came over to me again. She asked: "What's with you?" I thought she meant to ask what I was suffering from, since we were in a hospital, but this was not what she meant, she repeated the question: "What's with you?"

"I don't understand what you mean," I said.

Then she told me that for a long time she had been suffering form anxiety, and lately it had felt so bad that she couldn't sleep for one whole night for two months. "But when you were rolled into this room yesterday, something came along with you. I don't know what it was, but it was such a peace that came in here, which made all anxiety disappear, and I slept good all night through. So now I'm curious as to what's with you, " she repeated.

"It's Jesus!" I said, "Its Jesus." It's Him who came together with me in here yesterday. For I'm a Christian, and wherever I am, there He will be too."

This lady was not a Christian, and she had many questions. I didn't bring a Bible with me, as the admittance happened so quickly, but in the room lay a Bible that the Gideon Organization had put there. We picked it up and started reading. Many conversations happened during these days. I couldn't tell whether this lady received Jesus, but she had been given a choice.

Perhaps this was one of many encounters she would have to have before receiving Jesus. At least we both experienced that Jesus shows us that wherever you are as a Christian, there He will be as well.

When we accept Jesus as our Lord and Savior, we are hidden in Him.

In Colossians 3:4 it is written: *"When Christ, who is your life, appears, then you also will appear with him in glory." Christ, our life*. Wherever you are, there Jesus will also be.

Now Go

I was asked to preach one weekend at a campsite called Ildjarntun in Valdres, located in Central Norway. I felt at peace to say yes. When the time approached for the trip, I fell sick with fever and a sore throat. Since my voice is the instrument I use on a pulpit, I prayed to the Father, but didn't recover. Just before the weekend, I was again in prayer – should I cancel or should I go? I felt very bad about sending my regrets. Then I got a phone call with a greeting from a lady from Vestfold in the eastern part of Norway. She had no idea that I had fallen ill, but she had read my books and just wanted to greet me with Deuteronomy 31:8: *"The Lord himself goes before you and will be with you; he will never leave you nor forsake you. Do not be afraid; do not be discouraged."*

Then I received a text message from a lady from Nordfjord, in the western part of Norway, who had heard me preaching. Now she just wanted to send me a greeting from Exodus 32:34: *"Now go, lead the people to the place I spoke of, and my angel will go before you."*

So I went on the trip to Valdres, after all. On the day I left, I had no fever and my throat wasn't hurting anymore. I was able to stand and preach, but when I came home, I was tired and needed to rest.

In the book of Mark, we can read about Jesus sending His disciples out to preach. When they came back, He said to them: *"Come with me by yourselves to a quiet place and get some rest"* (Mark 6:31). Sometimes the days are such that we are sent out, and sometimes the

"The Lord sustains them on their sickbed and restores them from their bed of illness"

days are such that we simply lie there saved. He is with us always, and in Him I put my trust. He who says in the book of Matthew 28:18-20: *"All authority in heaven and on earth has been given to me. Therefore go and make disciples of all nations, baptizing them in the name of the Father and of the Son and of the Holy Spirit, and teaching them to obey everything I have commanded you. And surely I am with you always, to the very end of the age."*

Stand Firm!

Becoming older and weaker isn't easy. When the body starts ailing and doesn't function as before, considerable changes in life can occur. An elderly lady who is my interceder has gradually become confined to her bed. She can no longer attend meetings, listen to the preaching, and be a part of the fellowship, yet my bedridden interceder makes intercession for me every evening. And, she says, whenever she wakes up during the night and isn't able to sleep, she also prays for me. A greater gift couldn't have been given me.

I had been to Bergen and preached at a conference for the Interior Mission to Seamen (*Den Indre Sjoemannsmisjon*). Recordings of the sermons were made, and I asked if I could buy two sets of them. One for my bedridden interceder, and for me. They gave me both as a gift. When I came home and had some extra time one day, I called my interceder and thanked her for the prayer she had reminded the Lord with, and told her about the recordings she was going to get.

She told me that she had felt a little depressed today, and this she had said to her heavenly Father. Then she had been strongly reminded of a word she had read a couple of days before during her devotional time: *"Even to your old age and gray hairs I am he, I am he who will sustain you. I have made you and I will carry you; I will sustain you and I will rescue you"* (Isaiah 46:4).

This was comforting. The Lord would sustain her, but her thoughts were still a little heavy. Thus she was a little anxious. There it said: *"Do not be afraid. Stand firm and you will see the deliverance the Lord will bring you today"* Exodus 14:13. This gave her expectations of the Lord. She laid herself to rest, and waited for what He would send her on this day.

And just then I called, asking whether she would like to have these recordings from the meetings. "That was the Lord," she said, who came like this and showed her His care. She went on: "So this was how He wanted to come to me today. Yes, He came, just as He had promised."

To listen to the preaching of the Word is important for all of us. Thus it can be a substantial change to be bedridden with one's own thoughts. In 1 Peter 1:25, Peter says: *"... but the word of the Lord endures forever."*

Cassette tapes with preaching, CDs, Christian broadcasts on radio and TV can mean a lot for homes where sickness or other things hinder people from coming to a Christian community. In Romans 10:17, it says that faith comes *"from hearing the message, and the message is heard through the word about Christ."* The Word is with us and keeps us in the Lord Jesus Christ all the way home, thus: *"Let the message of Christ dwell among you richly"* (Colossians 3:16).

Waiting for the Lord

Waiting for the Lord can take time. There are times in life when we have to wait. Waiting for the Lord. We may be set aside due to sickness, or other things happen that make us wait. I had been having too much to do for some time. More than my health permitted, thus I was bedridden. There may be times when it feels good to rest, as it is a blessing to be set aside in quietness. However, there may also be times when this feels hard. This time I became discouraged. I placed it in the Father's hands, but the thoughts that took the courage away from me came around nonetheless. Even times of rest can strangely enough feel arduous.

Waiting for the Lord can involve a lot. For instance, everyday life may take its course, while you are waiting for an answer or a deliverance which you cannot see coming. This can take years. However, those who turn to the Lord never wait in vain. Indeed, it's Him who says in Jeremiah 31:9: *"...because I am Israel's father..."*

"The Lord sustains them on their sickbed and restores them from their bed of illness"

And just before this, He says: *"I will lead them beside streams of water…"* So there I lay, and could do nothing else.

Then one day a greeting came – from Isaiah 46:9-10: *"I am God, and there is none like me. I make known the end from the beginning, from ancient times, what is still to come. I say, 'My purpose will stand, and I will do all that I please.'"*

Just after that a greeting from a lady with the words from Isaiah 54:10 came on my cell phone: *"Though the mountains be shaken and the hills be removed, yet my unfailing love for you will not be shaken nor my covenant of peace be removed," says the Lord, who has compassion on you."*

Not long after, that very day, a third greeting came. Another lady had been reminded to call me with a greeting from Lamentations 3:5-26: *"The LORD is good to those whose hope is in him, to the one who seeks him; it is good to wait quietly for the salvation of the Lord."*

So the right truth over my life during this time was that I was in my heavenly Father's arms while the covenant of peace in the Lord Jesus Christ and His goodness surrounded me.

In my own eyes, and in the eyes of others, I was set aside, but was I really so?

C.H. Spurgeon, also known as the prince of preachers, once said it this way: *"One of the best ways the Lord can protect His people, is by making them strong in their inner being."*

So there I lay in the midst of the Lord's mercy as a saved person – waiting for days and days, when my body could function again. Maybe it is exactly in times of waiting that the Lord proclaims His grace over our lives so that we learn that our strength is indeed in Him, and in Him alone. He who tells us: *"My grace is sufficient for you, for my power is made perfect in weakness."* 2 Corinthians 12:9

"Whoever dwells in the shelter of the Most High" Psalm 91:1

I wasn't feeling well, tests were taken, and now I was facing more tests. My thoughts were many. At the same time, I learned that people we used to trust had let us down. Friends we thought were our friends, turned out not to be so. I went with all my pain to God, to Him who can enter into our lives in a wondrous way that transcends all our understanding – because He loves us. I went to Him who gave His only begotten Son so that whoever believes in Him should not perish but have everlasting life. In Him I trusted. And I prayed for help.

Then I received a text message from a lady in the United States who wanted to greet me with Psalm 91:1: *"Whoever sits in the shelter of the Most High….."* It didn't say *stand, walk, run,* work, but *sit* there and is saved. It said nothing about being in activity, but it said that it was the Most High who was active. I was only to sit still, only be with Him, and He would hide me. What a rest. The Lord would protect my life. Whether this meant going home now or later, the Lord would protect my life, which the whole psalm testified about. I gave thanks for the rest He gives by grace alone.

Oeyvind Brakvante, who was a fellow producer of the series, "Through the Bible," for a Norwegian Christian radio channel (*Kristen Riksradio*), had many listeners, and God used him as a tool in many people's lives. He once said: "I had to go through a difficult period of illness before I learned that He is the one who carries through it all. And so that I learned to thank Him for every day and for His grace."

Many suffer, have diseases, or are troubled by problems with relationships. In the midst of this situation, Jesus enters in. Jesus is there for us when we fall out. He is there when illness strikes and life becomes difficult. He is near to comfort and help. He is near to encourage and bless. He forgives and releases the one who comes to Him. Let us keep close to God. People can let you down, but the Lord's love is unchangeable. For, as it is written in the book of James 1:17: *"Every good and perfect gift is from above, coming down from the Father of the heavenly lights, who does not change like shifting shadows."* The one who dwells in the shelter of the Most High: *"He is my refuge and my fortress, my God, in whom I trust"* (Psalm 91:2).

"The Lord sustains them on their sickbed and restores them from their bed of illness"

God is Able to Bless You Abundantly

After several doses of penicillin, my stomach didn't function as it should, and I needed to see the doctor. In my book, *In God's Hand,* I've written about my intolerance to milk, a condition that can be a little troublesome, especially when I'm out traveling. In addition to getting medical assistance, I also got intercession for these conditions. For God can heal, also through prayers. He also heals through health personnel – God works in many ways. I recovered, but it went very slowly. After a while, I could from time to time eat more milk products, a little cheese and a little ice cream. Maybe I will never fully recover while here on earth, but one day at home, all diseases and suffering will be wiped away. In the meantime, my everyday life has improved, although some backlashes occur now and then.

One day when I had promised to preach at two different places with only a few days in between, and I wasn't feeling well, I felt unsure whether this would work out. I lay flat out with a headache, an upset stomach, and I was feeling exhausted.

Then I went in prayer to the Father: would He help me recover? Would He grant me wisdom to see what He wanted me to see in this situation? Perhaps I had said yes one too many times? Should I send my regrets?

I lay down to rest while hoping and waiting for an answer. I knew the Father would give me everything I would need if He wanted me to go.

Then I received a text message from a lady who wanted to greet me with some words from the Bible. She hoped it would fit in my situation. It was taken from 2 Corinthians 9:8: *"And God is able to bless you abundantly, so that in all things at all times, having all that you need, you will abound in every good work."*

This gave peace to restless thoughts. I felt at peace not to send my regrets but to wait for the Lord. We can gain strength when we read about how others previously have put their trust in God and His promises. This can give us courage in our everyday life. Paul writes in Romans 4:21 about Abraham having been promised a son in his old age, with his wife aged ninety, how Abraham *"being fully persuaded that God had power to do what he had promised."*

The Lord never leaves us alone, we don't need to walk in our own strength. So upon receiving these words, I felt at peace and rested, confident that the Father would give me what I needed. And when the time came for the meetings, I gained strength to go. In 2 Corinthians 6:16, the Lord says: *"I will live with them and walk among them, and I will be their God, and they will be my people."*

Cry Unto Me

When growing up, my grandpa, my mother's father, wasn't a believer. What I remember most vividly about him was his great sense of justice. My first memory regarding this was when the extended family was gathered in Grandpa's house. It was mealtime and I was small and sitting in a cardboard box on the floor, playing. The other kids, who were older, were allowed to sit by the table. I remember a discussion arose from this. Grandpa wanted me at the table, the others said I was too small. There was a set of children-sized knife and spoon with light blue handles. Then he lifted me up unto his lap, and I was a part of the fellowship at the table. I remember my heart was overwhelmed by this gift that was so nice.

When Grandpa was around fifty years old, he got cardiac problems for the first time. Several times he had to be admitted to the hospital in acute condition. He was still a non-believer. Later when he had reached seventy-two years of age, he was again rushed to the hospital in an ambulance. He was very weak and fell into a coma.

At home we went into prayer. My parents were believers, and they cried out for salvation for Grandpa, that God somehow had to intervene. They put their trust in the words in Jeremiah 33:2-3: *"This is what the Lord says, he who made the earth, the Lord who formed it and established it – the Lord is his name: 'Call to me and I will answer you and tell you great and unsearchable things you do not know.'"*

Grandma and our family took turns on watching over him. One day when Mother and my grandma were with him, they wanted to try to lift him up a little in the bed. He lay with a backrest, a little tilted upwards with his upper part of the body, and now he had slid a little

"The Lord sustains them on their sickbed and restores them from their bed of illness"

down in the bed. They went on one side each of his bed and tried to lift him, but this wasn't an easy thing to do because he was a big man. While they were struggling with this, the hospital priest, Magnus Nymann, came suddenly into the room. (When I attended church in my youth in Grim Church in Kristiansand, he was a pastor there. A fine Christian man. During his ministry there was a revival among the youth.) He saw that they were struggling, and asked whether he could help. Grandpa was still in a coma. Just as Nymann lifted Grandpa up, he said to him: "God bless you." Then Grandpa opened his eyes, looked at Nymann and said loudly and clearly: "Yes," before falling back into his unconscious condition.

The following day, Grandpa woke up. He was completely changed. He had received Jesus. He was seventy-two years old and newly saved. God had heard our prayers and answered in an extraordinary way.

What happened when Nymann blessed Grandpa? Was that when he met Jesus? We don't know, but we do know that when he woke up, he was saved, for this he himself testified about. And we had him for another five weeks. For these five weeks, he was a transformed man we spent time with. We had many good conversations about spiritual things. Psalm 100 was Grandpa's psalm during this time:

> *"A psalm. For giving grateful praise. Shout for joy to the Lord, all the earth. Worship the Lord with gladness; come before him with joyful songs. Know that the Lord is God. It is he who made us, and we are his; we are his people, the sheep of his pasture. Enter his gates with thanksgiving and his courts with praise; give thanks to him and praise his name. For the Lord is good and his love endures forever; his faithfulness continues through all generations."*

One of Grandpa's neighbors was Bible school teacher Simon Roeksland. They had often run into each other as neighbors. However, Grandpa was probably not always easy to deal with. A lot of intercession took place around him, and it can be hard to kick against the goads. Meeting Christians who give a fragrance of the Lord Jesus can make called people uneasy until they find peace with God.

Jesus met Paul this way when he was resisting his call. *"...I heard a voice saying to me in Aramaic, 'Saul, Saul, why do you persecute me? It is hard for you to kick against the goads.' Then I asked, 'Who are you, Lord?' 'I am Jesus, whom you are persecuting,' the Lord replied."* Acts 26:14-15

When Grandpa was saved, Roeksland heard about it and went to visit him. Afterwards he said that upon entering the room, he could feel that Jesus was already there. He said: "The Spirit of God was perceptibly present."

This conversation was different from all the other conversations these two neighbors had had. Not many days later, Grandpa went home to Jesus while resting.

Perhaps you too have someone you pray for in your family who isn't saved. In that case, I wish to hand you these words on the way: "This is what the Lord says, he who made the earth, the Lord who formed it and established it—the Lord is his name: 'Call to me and I will answer you and tell you great and unsearchable things you do not know.'"

Messianic Believers

The first time I met Brit Svanhild BenShitrit Maestad, was in Soegne some fifteen years ago. She was a Christian girl who had married a non-believing Jew, Michael BenShitrit. He was born and raised in Israel while she was born and raised in Norway. Since she was a Christian girl, she prayed faithfully that her husband must see who Jesus is, and live accordingly. After a while, they had three children and settled down in Soegne. Michael's life changed when he was introduced into a different culture and a foreign country. He himself tells:

I was born and raised in Israel, and as a kid I was taught the Torah and the Old Testament. My family was an ordinary Jewish family that observed the Sabbath and celebrated the Jewish holy days. But I rebelled against this. By and by I distanced myself completely from all the rules that were imposed on the Jews. And the further I distanced myself, the further I came away from everything

"The Lord sustains them on their sickbed and restores them from their bed of illness"

---

called faith. Eventually, I didn't believe in any Jewish God. I became an Atheist.

I worked at a *kibbutz* – a collective where we live and work in fellowship. This is very common in many places in Israel. Youth and grownups from all over the world come to experience this special way of living and working. They work in a kibbutz for some weeks or months or a whole year. One day a Norwegian girl came to the kibbutz. That was Brit. We worked together and got to know each other. After a while, we also started meeting in our leisure time.

But then the day came when she had to leave for Norway – her stay was over. Many thoughts and feelings occurred. When she was gone, I missed her so much that I eventually packed my suitcase and went after her to a foreign country and a foreign culture.

Brit was raised in a Christian home. She also had a grandmother who prayed for all the children, grandchildren and their families, so when I started talking about getting married, this was difficult for Brit. Could she marry someone with whom she didn't share the faith? Someone who didn't believe there is a God? Her questions and prayers were many, but finally she ended up with a yes.

The day we married, she got a word from the Bible with a special promise. It was from Jeremiah 29:11: *"For I know the plans I have for you," declares the Lord, "plans to prosper you and not to harm you, plans to give you hope and a future."* This gave her peace in her heart, she said.

Friends and family in Norway prayed for us. I received a Bible in Hebrew, my mother tongue, as a gift. I ended up joining Brit at Christian meetings, but only to be together with her.

We got Christian neighbors and friends. Brit participated in a prayer group that prayed for all the neighbors, including me. I couldn't be a part of the prayer group since we didn't share the faith. After a while, I started realizing that I lacked something, and I started wondering whether the God they prayed to was the same as the one I had learnt about in my childhood. I was invited to a Bible group. Out of pure curiosity I accepted, for my thoughts had gradually become many. In the Bible group we started reading from the book of Matthew together. When we came to Matthew 7:13-14, we read: *"Enter through the narrow gate. For wide is the gate and broad is the road that leads to destruction, and many enter through it. But small is the gate and narrow the road that leads to life, and only a few find it."* When we read this, I felt a cry in my heart after finding this road and this gate.

Some time later, we came to chapter 13 in Matthew and verses 40 through 43. There I noticed in particular verse 42, where it is written: *"They will throw them into the blazing furnace, where there will be weeping and gnashing of teeth."* This scared me.

That night I couldn't get peace. I couldn't go to sleep. Brit went to bed, but I remained sitting and reading the Bible. As the night drew on, I started praying: *Where are you, God?*

Early in the morning when I was totally exhausted, so exhausted after the battle that night, I prayed: *God, how shall I find you?*

Then, suddenly, Jesus stood before me. It was overwhelming. I felt paralyzed. Jesus himself was standing there in the room in a mighty light, and in the midst of it all was a wondrous peace. In Hebrew, my mother tongue, he said to me: "I know about your battle, and wanted to see how much you could stand. I couldn't come until you wanted me a hundred percent, but now I know that you want to be with me. That's why I have come to you now."

Jesus stood there and talked to me, me who didn't even want to believe he existed! He came to me, and then it was all over. With it came an indescribable peace. It was true. God was real. When I finally ducked under the sheets, I slept so well. I had met Jesus. The Messiah.

Helge Hoeyland was the minister in Sogne. He and his wife Liv had spent many years in Israel in connection with a work assignment in a congregation in Haifa. Thus they were very familiar with the country, the culture and the Jewish faith. I had many conversations with Helge, and he helped me to understand a little more. He spoke Hebrew, which was a great help to me. I came to know that the God I had now met was the same God I had grown up with in Israel. I learned about a good God, a loving God, a God who loves everyone. This was a new realization. God wasn't strict and didn't have so many rules that had been hammered in during my childhood and adolescence. God was good.

This lesson resulted in my baptism, but before the baptism we traveled to Israel to tell my family what I had experienced, and that I

"The Lord sustains them on their sickbed and restores them from their bed of illness"

---

now believed in Yesuha Hamashiach (Jesus the Messiah). We wanted to tell them that Jesus was the Messiah, the risen.

It became a thrilling trip. I felt very uncertain as to how my family would react. It turned out that Mother was open to my new faith. She said that as long as it was good for me, it was good for her. But Father reacted differently. We had a painful conversation in which Father furiously declared that since I chose this faith, I was a "goy," a heathen, and he would no longer consider me his son. I was expelled from my family, which was very painful. I felt as if I lost everything in Israel. As a result of the conversation with my father, I also lost contact with other family members that I previously had stayed in touch with. It hurts to think back at the time that followed. My own father would no longer acknowledge me, his own son. Had I known this in advance, would I then have become a Christian? The answer is yes. Jesus was alive, this was the truth, and I could never go back on that. Never. I had come "home" and had been set free. Only the truth sets free.

It lasted some months before my father wanted to contact me again. He became seriously ill, and we traveled to Israel. The time of his illness lasted for a long time, one and a half years. During this time, we had many more trips to Israel. I prayed to God that I could be in Israel with him when he died. Eventually, he fell into a coma. I was sitting beside him, alone on the last morning of his life. I thank God for giving me this opportunity. I had brought my Bible in Hebrew, and I sat and read to him from the book of Psalms there by his sickbed. Then I prayed out loud that Jesus must take him himself. When I prayed this, he suddenly opened his eyes and looked at me, then he passed away peacefully. I hope he also got to meet Jesus.

Today I live as a Messianic-believing Jew in Norway. We have found our congregation, and as a family we're happy there. I have experienced that prayer is important, and my whole life testifies about this. I'm so grateful that I've found Jesus, he who is Yesuha Hamashiach. There was truth in the word that Brit got on our wedding day from Jeremiah 29:11: *"For I know the plans I have for you," declares the Lord, "plans to prosper you and not to harm you, plans to give you hope and a future."*

The Two Jars

Have you ever wondered why some are sick while others are healthy? Have you been thinking that it's the healthy ones that God can make use of? At least more and better. It's not unusual to think like this, however, luckily the Lord Jesus shows us that this isn't the whole picture. Paul writes in 2 Corinthians 4:7: *"But we have this treasure in jars of clay to show that this all-surpassing power is from God and not from us."*

Many times I've been blessed through people who are fragile jars. They reflect God's greatness through their weakness. Job, who experienced much suffering, said to God: *"I know that you can do all things; no purpose of yours can be thwarted."* Job 42:2

Having been through a lot of illness, I totally agree with Job. The Lord Jesus doesn't look for what you are, but for what He can do with you with His nail-pierced hands. He performs His heavenly work in the midst of inferiority complexes, anxiety, poor health, and painful life situations. He says: *"My grace is sufficient for you, for my power is made perfect in weakness."* 2 Corinthians 12:9

Once I was going to preach on a weekend in eastern Norway. As the day approached, my health wasn't at its best, so I prayed to the Father for help. Then a greeting came in the mail from Eva Flaa in Kristiansand, who was struggling with illness herself. She wanted to remind me with the words from Micah 2:13: *"The One who breaks open the way will go up before them; they will break through the gate and go out. Their King will pass through before them, the Lord at their head."* That word carried me through the weekend, and I am so grateful that I went. Despite the fragile jar, it became a blessed weekend. Jesus was there.

Have you ever felt like a fragile jar? To me, the story about the servant with the two jars has often been of help and comfort.

A servant had two large jars that he used to bring water in to his master's house; they hung one on each end on a long yoke. One of the jars had a crack, and every time the servant completed the long walk from the creek to his master's house, the cracked jar was only half-full. The other jar was perfect and full of water. Thus the servant delivered one and a half jars of water to his master every day.

"The Lord sustains them on their sickbed and restores them from their bed of illness"

The perfect jar was proud of what it accomplished, but the cracked jar was ashamed that it wasn't good enough, that it only accomplished half of what it was made for.

After two years of failure and defeat, the cracked jar one day said to the servant: "I'm ashamed of myself, and I want to apologize." "What are you ashamed of?" the servant asked. The jar said: "During these two years I've only managed to deliver half of the content because the crack in my side makes the water leak all the way up to your master's house. And because of my defects you don't get the total profit from your work." The servant replied: "When we now go back to my master's house, I want you to notice the beautiful flowers alongside the path."

On the way home, the cracked jar noticed all the beautiful flowers that grew alongside the path. When they reached the house, the servant said to the jar: "Did you notice that the flowers are only green on your side of the path, and not on the other jar's side? This is because I've always known about your defect, and I've made use of it. I sowed flower seeds on your side of the path, and every day when we wander back from the creek, you've watered them. And for two years I've been able to pick beautiful flowers to decorate my master's table with. "

In 2 Corinthians 12:9, the Lord teaches: *"... my power is made perfect in weakness."* Your weakness is God's opportunity, He has good plans for you as well. He makes use of you where the perfect jar is unusable. Many of us have injuries and weaknesses, but if we place ourselves at the Lord's disposal, just as we are, He can make use of our weaknesses to decorate our heavenly Father's table. He who says: *My grace is sufficient for you, for my power is made perfect in weakness.*

"...IN QUIETNESS AND TRUST IS YOUR STRENGTH"
Isaiah 30:15

"He giveth, and giveth, and giveth again"

Again, there have been many meetings. The strength isn't always that great, and the boundary you shouldn't cross isn't always so easy to see. Now I was exhausted and needed to rest.

To rest with the Lord is good for spirit, soul and body. In His presence we can gain new strength from His sources. Everybody needs the rest that the Lord gives. In Psalm 23, David testifies about his walk with the Lord and what he experiences when he let the Lord be the shepherd. He wrote: *"…he leads me beside quiet waters."*

Now I was in need of quiet waters. I lay there and could do nothing else – so tired, so tired. Then a greeting came in the door from Toril Boen. She had heard me preach at a women's conference at a weekend in Stavanger on the west coast of Norway, and now she wanted to give me a greeting and thanks through a letter and a gift. Inside the gift was a beautiful shawl. But she had also included a song. She wrote that she had been reminded to send me this song, and indeed it came at the right time. It had the fragrance of Jesus. It had been jotted down by memory, wrote Toril, and she didn't know who was the poet behind it. I called my friend Solveig Soerli, who has a ministry in singing for Jesus. She has extended knowledge on many different songs.

Solveig knew the song was written by A. J. Flint, and translated from English to Swedish by Ivar Lindestad.

He Giveth More Grace
He giveth more grace as our burdens grow greater,
He sendeth more strength as our labors increase;

To added afflictions He addeth His mercy,
To multiplied trials He multiplies peace.

When we have exhausted our store of endurance,
When our strength has failed ere the day is half done,
When we reach the end of our hoarded resources
Our Father's full giving is only begun.

Fear not that thy need shall exceed His provision,
Our God ever yearns His resources to share
Lean hard on the arm everlasting, availing;
The Father both thee and thy load will upbear.

His love has no limits, His grace has no measure,
His power no boundary known unto men;
For out of His infinite riches in Jesus
He giveth, and giveth, and giveth again.

When I had read the song, I rested again with new courage, for as it said: "He giveth, and giveth, and giveth again." Perhaps you who read this also needed this song greeting today. Accept it, and don't be afraid, for the Lord is mighty to make *"...water will gush forth in the wilderness and streams in the desert"* (Isaiah 35:6). When we rest, it may take some time, but after a while we will see these remarkable things which so many before us have seen and testified about, that *"...the streams of God are filled with water"* (Psalm 65:9).

"...he carries them close to his heart" Isaiah 40:11

Sometimes it is as if everything comes at the same time. Many things can be hard to deal with, such is life. But when you get everything at the same time in your lap, the burden may seem pretty insuperable. Now I had promised to write and record five devotions for *Norea Radio* (a Norwegian Christian broadcaster), preaching assignments were waiting for me, and many wanted to see me for intercession and counseling. I was tired and struggling with headache – how was I to manage it all? I prayed to the Father for help and wisdom.

I said: Today I'm in need of resting at Your heart. Just to be a child and receive care while You take care of all of this. Then I received a text message from Randi Vorhaug in Arendal in southern Norway. She wrote that she really felt as if Jesus wanted to give me verse 11 from Isaiah 40: *"...and he carries them close to his heart"* – she hoped it fit. My word, what a change it caused! This gave joy and a sense of being cared for.

Some twenty minutes later, another text came, this time from Olaug Aa from Bryggja in the west of Norway. She wrote: "I was strongly reminded that you should have this from Deuteronomy 33:12: *"...the one the Lord loves rests between his shoulders."*

Then Nina Wullum called from Horten in eastern Norway. She just wanted to give me my own poem "Exactly you," she said, as a greeting this day. Oh, wonderful Father. I had to sit down and read the words and the poem I had been given over and over again.

Exactly you
I want you to know
that the Lord carries
exactly you,
close to His heart.

He has placed you
most closely
against His beating heart,
for that is when He sees you
the best.

And His loving eyes
they flow with tenderness,
down to you
because you are indeed
His child.

He protects you,
lets you rest and grow,
then He says to you:
My child, never forget
that the battle is Mine
and Mine alone.
You may rest
in confidence with Me
while I will fight
also for you.

I thanked the Father in prayer. He often confirms through two or three witnesses. Once again, I was given the rest and care that only He can give. Even though I needed pills to get rid of the headache, I learned that I could rest through the greetings I received. It is said that in the center of a hurricane it is completely still. The rest and the quietness that the Lord gives, are sometimes such a center.

Let us turn to Him who Nahum writes about: *"His way is in the whirlwind and the storm, and clouds are the dust of his feet... The Lord is good, a refuge in times of trouble. He cares for those who trust in him"* (Nahum 1:3 and 7).

A Lesson Learned

In Matthew 6:33, Jesus says: *"But seek first his kingdom and his righteousness, and all these things will be given to you as well."* To seek God first isn't always that easy. Often times we find our own solutions, and act accordingly. But here Jesus talks about seeking God's Kingdom first. A part of my ministry has been serving in teams in different contexts. Once, in one of the teams, something happened that forced us to make a difficult decision.

One person spoke falsely about the evangelization work we were in the midst of, and spread this lie further. Should we confront the person in question, or should we keep quiet about it? Spiritual warfare is a part of ministering, and knowing how to react when the attacks come constantly involves praying to God about guidance in every situation.

"...in quietness and trust is your strength"

We agreed to pray to God for wisdom in this situation. This was one Thursday evening. The following morning, one text message after the other ticked in on my cell phone from the other members of the team. All but one agreed to keep quiet. The other wrote that we should not put up with this, that this was unfair and needed to be brought up with the person in question.

Then suddenly another text message ticked in from a lady who knew nothing about our dilemma. She wrote that she wanted to greet me with the words from Exodus 14:13-14: *"Moses answered the people, 'Do not be afraid. Stand firm and you will see the deliverance the Lord will bring you today. The Egyptians you see today you will never see again. The Lord will fight for you; you need only to be still.'"* I forwarded this word to the others, and we agreed to keep quiet and let the Lord fight.

Some days later, the one in the team who had wished to tell about the matter and not keep quiet came and said: "I got a real lesson learned that day when we received the word about keeping quiet and let the Lord fight. You see, I didn't pray over the matter, something that I obviously should've done. I experienced what had happened as unfair and just made the decision in pure anger over the injustice that had been committed, and sent you the text message without having prayed first. This became a lesson learned for me."

When I was at Lindisfarne, the small tidal island off the northeast coast of England, I came across some texts. One of them was by Mother Teresa. I translated it into Norwegian. The text is about dearly bought experiences on the walk with the Lord.

"Anyway"
by Mother Teresa

People are often unreasonable,
illogical and self-centered;
Forgive them anyway.

If you are kind,
people may accuse you
of selfish, ulterior motives;

You are never alone

Be kind anyway.

If you are successful,
you will win some false friends
and some true enemies;
Succeed anyway.

If you are honest and frank,
people may cheat you;
Be honest and frank anyway.

What you spend years building,
someone could destroy overnight;
Build anyway.

If you find serenity and happiness,
they may be jealous;
Be happy anyway.

The good you do today,
people will often forget tomorrow;
Do good anyway.

Give the world the best you have,
and it may never be enough;
Give the world the best you've got anyway.

You see, in the final analysis,
it is between you and your God;
It was never between you and them anyway.

In Colossians 3:23, Paul says it this way: *"Whatever you do, work at it with all your heart, as working for the Lord, not for human masters."*

"...in quietness and trust is your strength"

Give yourself time for food and rest

I was preaching at a community center in a village I had never visited before. After the sermon, there was time for testimonies. Then a young lady stood up. She told that for some time ago she didn't want to live any longer. She had experienced a lot of sorrow, and life became difficult for her. But then she was stopped by two of my poems. The poems were "Give yourself" and "Take food."

Give yourself
Give
yourself
time.
Give yourself
time
for food
and rest.

Behold,
there is honey
on the ground.

Give yourself
time
to eat.

Behold,
there is quite a stream
of honey.

Reach out your staff,
dip it in honey
and bring it to your mouth.

Then
your eyes
will be clear.

Take food
When you're on the road
or sit in your house,
take food.

If you go without food,
I'm asking you:
Take food.
For this runs along with
your salvation.

Thank God
before the eyes of everybody.
Break the bread
and start eating.

Then others too
will take courage
so that they themselves
can take food.

Then all of you
will take new courage.

She told us that these poems had been her rescue. She experienced that they spoke to her that she had to take bread and honey, which are an image of God's word.

The day after, a lady came to visit and told her that she had been strongly reminded by the Lord to give her a gift. She knew nothing about what had happened. Then she handed her a basket with bread and honey.

When I wrote these poems, I had no idea that they could be used in such a way by the Lord. In Psalm 145:3, it is written: *"Great is the Lord and most worthy of praise; his greatness no one can fathom."* Indeed, truly His greatness no one can fathom.

What this fine young lady testified about yet again made me realize that it's all about sowing out what we are given from Him – and then leave the rest to Him. In 1 Corinthians 3:6-7, Paul says: *"I planted the seed, Apollos watered it, but God has been making it grow. So neither the one who plants nor the one who waters is anything, but only God, who makes things grow."*

"THEREFORE I TELL YOU, DO NOT WORRY ABOUT YOUR LIFE, WHAT YOU WILL EAT OR DRINK…"
Matthew 6:25

Abundance on the stairs

Christmas was approaching, and I had gotten several assignments. Some of those who had asked me for preaching didn't offer any payment for the assignments, but I went nevertheless. Perhaps now, you might say that we have received it for nothing, and shall give it for nothing. However, it's also written that a worker deserves his or her wages. In any case, I think that God has called me, and thus I leave it all to Him.

When one night I came home late with a flower as the payment, my husband said that we had to look at this evening as a part of the tithe. I placed it in Father's hands, and asked Him to look after us the way He thought the best. Then we went to bed.

The following morning when I woke up, I saw two large gifts on the table in the living room next to the flower I had received at the meeting the previous evening. They were elegantly wrapped in Cellophane.

In one of them I found a basket with seven breads: two spelt breads, two oatmeal breads, two rye breads, and one bread with walnuts and wheat, all decorated with pretty ribbons and each with a Bible verse attached to it. There was an angel hanging on the basket with an envelope and a large lilac heart with the words from Deuteronomy 28:5-14, that begin like this: *"Your basket and your kneading trough will be blessed. You will be blessed when you come in and blessed when you go out."* And inside the envelope was the exact amount I should've received in salary.

Inside the other gift were three cookie boxes full of homemade cookies. All the boxes had Bible verses attached. It was an abundance of gifts, but no sender. I had to call my husband, who had already gone to work, and ask what this was. He told me that when he walked out on the stairs in the morning, the gifts were already there. He didn't know who the giver was either.

We were so happy for the gifts we had received, and rejoicing and thanksgiving followed to the Father who had blessed us so richly. The Bible verses were also a great blessing as the breads and cakes were gradually eaten in the days that followed.

Even to this day, the giver hasn't been heard from.

That very morning when this happened, I received a text message with the words from Matthew 7:7-8: *"Ask and it will be given to you; seek and you will find; knock and the door will be opened to you. For everyone who asks receives; the one who seeks finds; and to the one who knocks, the door will be opened."*

"Hardangerlefser"

The first Christmas after we moved down to Kristiansand and I had newly undergone surgery, my strength didn't suffice for the Christmas preparations. My thoughts wandered to the Christmas baking. The only thing I wished for was *Hardangerlefse* (thin pastry usually served folded and spread with butter, cinnamon and sugar). I decided to place this matter with Father.

I knew that I couldn't bake it myself, but then I also knew that I could ask for anything. At the same time, I thought that even though there might not be any "lefser," we would still have a nice Christmas. It was around noon on a Wednesday before Christmas that I prayed this prayer.

The same afternoon, around 3:30 pm, the doorbell rang.

It was Arhild Aasland from Finsland north of Kristiansand who stopped by. She told me that she really wanted to give me a Christmas present, but she didn't know what it should be, and thus had sought God for advice in prayer. Then it came to her that she should make me "hardangerlefser," and now she came with a plastic bag full of freshly baked "lefser" for me.

"Therefore I tell you, do not worry about your life, what you will eat or drink..."

They had been baked that very Wednesday. However, on Monday she had already bought what she needed to bake. What a Father we have! He is the one it is written about in Isaiah 65:24: *"Before they call I will answer; while they are still speaking I will hear."*

Cake with the Coffee

We had a phone call announcing visitors. This we appreciated very much. Some would come this day, and some the day after. But I had no cake. I'm sure many would claim that this doesn't matter! No, not necessarily so, however, it's nice to have something to enjoy with the coffee. My husband was out with the car to get something, so I was alone. I could've made a cake, but I was so tired and worn. Thus I prayed to Father whether He could help me. I told Him just as it was, that I was expecting guests, was tired and lacked a cake.

This was in the morning, and I did no more with that matter. In the afternoon I received a phone call from a lady who told me that she had five packages of "hardangerlefser" that she wondered whether I'd like to have. If I wanted them, I could have them, but we had to pick them up at her place. Preferably the same day.

I thanked her and told her about my prayer the same morning. We both thanked the Father.

I called my husband to find out whether he was close to where she lived. It turned out that from where he was, he just had to turn off the road right afterwards to get to her place. Everything turned out to be a blessing. And we had cake with the coffee both days.

We can go to the Lord with even the most insignificant things. Let us turn to Him with our days and our lives. For it is He and He alone who blesses. He is mighty, and mighty to heal as well. He could've given me strength and good health to bake that day, but instead He used one of His children to bless us. God is good. All the time. In Psalm 115:12 it is written: *"The Lord remembers us and will bless us."*

WITH JESUS IN HUNGARY

Eger in Hungary

To be a freelance preacher can be lonely, but it can also be exciting and varied. One day I was asked by Lars Dahle, the president and the associate professor at Gimlekollen School of Journalism and Communication (GSJC), to join a group of Norwegians going to Eger in Hungary to attend the European Leadership Forum convention.

According to the program, the convention was meant to provide a bridge between God's global resources and local leaders from all over Europe. We could sit and listen to the world's best professors and teachers. There would be evangelic seminars and Bible studies. We would be taught in apologetics, leadership, and art and development by churches and congregations. The topics would be extensive – such as media communication and evangelization. The speakers and the lecturers were among the best in their fields: professors in theology, psychiatry, and so forth.

I prayed to God whether I could go. And should I go, I also prayed for financial means for the trip. What did He think about this matter? Was this prepared in advance for my walk?

A few days later, a lady called. She asked whether I was going to participate in a course soon? In that case, she wanted to pay for it. She had been reminded by the Lord, she said. I told her that I was praying for this, and that I felt at peace to go, but my aim was Hungary, and tickets and food and lodging would total around NOK 8,000 (about USD 1,320).

"I'm paying," she said, and added: "If it would've cost NOK 10,000 (about USD 1,650) I would've paid that as well."

So I went to Eger. And what a trip! What an experience! The first evening when I was sitting at the dinner table in the hotel, my tears of joy were running for what God let me experience.

I had been enrolled in a seminar for Christian counselors. Dr. Richard Winter from England was the leader for this. He was a psychiatrist and a professor in practical theology. It was moving to listen to his seminar about "Forgiving the unforgivable." I myself had preached over this "Forgiveness" topic several times, so this was even more interesting for me.

Every morning began with prayer and Bible class. These Bible classes were held by Lindsay Brown who has, among other things, been the European leader of the International Fellowship of Evangelical Students (IFES). One morning he preached over chapter 3 in Paul's letter to the Colossians. We are hidden in Christ in our faith in Him, Paul writes. Our future is secured, but we still need to walk in His light with our lives since we're not there yet. Our place in heaven has been reserved, but we still struggle as long as we are here on earth. Because we live in a fallen world.

This means that, among other things, we learn about forgiveness of our own sins, and about forgiving our fellow humans. In verse 13, it says: *"Bear with each other and forgive one another if any of you has a grievance against someone. Forgive as the Lord forgave you."*

Lindsay Brown told us that in a university in China, the authorities had planted a spy among the Christian students. Everybody knew who he was, but the Christians decided to live the Christian life they were called to, and to love him. The students had learned to live their lives in the presence of the Lord. They walked in accordance with His word just as Paul writes in Colossians 3:12-14 and 17: *"...as God's chosen people, holy and dearly loved, clothe yourselves with compassion, kindness, humility, gentleness and patience. Bear with each other and forgive one another if any of you has a grievance against someone. Forgive as the Lord forgave you. And over all these virtues put on love, which binds them all together in perfect unity... And whatever you do, whether in word or deed, do it all in the name of the Lord Jesus, giving thanks to God the Father through him."* After a year, the spy became a Christian. He said: "They loved me so much that my heart melted." In Colossians 3:23, Paul writes: *"Whatever you do, work at it with all your heart, as working for the Lord, not for human masters…"*

"I've been waiting for this"

During my stay in Eger in Hungary, I received a text message from a lady in Norway one day. She wrote that she had been reminded to tell me that there was someone there who needed me. I thought to myself that those people surrounding me really seemed so trained and educated, however I said to the Father that, "If You wish to use me for something here, then lead me step by step."

That evening, I was reminded to give a lady a word from the Bible. She was from Romania and worked as a psychotherapist. I felt a little unsure. Could I simply walk over to her with a verse from the Bible? Would she understand? Or would she think I was a little weird walking around handing out Bible verses to strangers? I hesitated in doing this, and thought that it had been easier to come with a greeting to a pastor or a priest. They would probably understand such things better.

I hesitated a lot, and didn't give her the word the following day. When the evening came, I was again reminded to give her this greeting. More strongly this time than the previous evening. Early the next morning, I brought my Bible to breakfast, and when I found her I went over to her and gave her the word.

She picked up her own Bible in her mother language. She was so happy and spontaneously exclaimed: "I've been waiting for this during the whole convention. I've been waiting and waiting. Finally it came!" She repeated this several times while thanking me. It turned out that she was traveling home a little earlier than the rest of us, just after this breakfast.

The Lord is wondrous. Peter writes: *"Each of you should use whatever gift you have received to serve others, as faithful stewards of God's grace in its various forms"* (1 Peter 4:10). I had to confess to the Lord how hard it had been for me to be obedient. It wasn't the first time I had to confess like this, and certainly not the last time.

My thanks went to the Father for what I got to see that He did there at the breakfast table. He who is mighty to equip us and work in us, so that His goodness and love will be visible among us.

Paul expresses it this way: *"Now may the God of peace, who through the blood of the eternal covenant brought back from the dead our Lord Jesus, that great Shepherd of the sheep, equip you with everything good for doing his will, and may he work in us what is pleasing to him, through Jesus Christ, to whom be glory for ever and ever. Amen"* (Hebrews 13:20-21).

"...do not let your hands hang limp" Zephaniah 3:16

On the final morning at the convention in Eger, Dr. Richard Winter sent us out with these words from Isaiah 61:1-3: *"The Spirit of the Sovereign LORD is on me, because the Lord has anointed me to proclaim good news to the poor. He has sent me to bind up the brokenhearted, to proclaim freedom for the captives and release from darkness for the prisoners, to proclaim the year of the Lord's favor and the day of vengeance of our God, to comfort all who mourn, and provide for those who grieve in Zion— to bestow on them a crown of beauty instead of ashes, the oil of joy instead of mourning, and a garment of praise instead of a spirit of despair. They will be called oaks of righteousness, a planting of the Lord for the display of his splendor."*

Dr. Winter encouraged us to go out to people with a good message. "When you walk out among people, when you meet the miserable, then you have a good message to tell them. He sends you out to bandage the wounds that have been inflicted on so many people and their hearts. And to help those who are in captivity and release those who are bound.

"All of those who are tied so that they are not free, release them and let them go. The Lord can make use of them. And tell them that one day the day of vengeance of our God will come. All the injustice that has been done to them, has been seen. One day…

"Go and comfort the mourning. Give them hope in the midst of all their days that will weigh them down. Take part in the pouring out of the oil of joy *in Christ* to them.

"And to the powerless, to all those who have been deprived of their power and dignity in their lives, so they have lost their courage, give them hope. Give them to drink from the Lord's water wells *in Christ*.

"Tell them that they are to be called by their rightful names, the oaks of righteousness. Go out with healing and a good message. Preach to them that they are a planting of the Lord for the display of his splendor."

These were powerful words to bring along on the journey. But I thought to myself that this applies more to the others than me. They were all so clever, and they would certainly manage this. I was more in doubt when it came to myself. But I placed my thoughts in the hands of the Lord, and prayed that His will must be done in everything.

When I came home to Norway, a text message ticked in on my cell phone from a lady who had been reminded to give me some words. She hoped they fit. The words where exactly the same as the ones we had been sent out with the day before from Isaiah 61:1-3.

My heart was filled with joy and wonder. She also greeted me with a word from Zephaniah 3:16: *"On that day they will say to Jerusalem, 'Do not fear, Zion; do not let your hands hang limp.'"*

Today you who read or hear this can also take these words with you on the way.

Sometimes I stop and ponder how we cannot fathom with our own intellect what a mighty and good God we have. The heavens and the highest heavens cannot contain Him, and yet He came to us.

The prophet Isaiah writes in chapter 6:1-4: *"In the year that King Uzziah died, I saw the Lord, high and exalted, seated on a throne; and the train of his robe filled the temple. Above him were seraphim, each with six wings: With two wings they covered their faces, with two they covered their feet, and with two they were flying. And they were calling to one another: 'Holy, holy, holy is the Lord Almighty; the whole earth is full of his glory.' At the sound of their voices the doorposts and thresholds shook and the temple was filled with smoke."*

In verse 8, the Lord calls on the ones who want to go with His word. *"Then I heard the voice of the Lord saying, 'Whom shall I send? And who will go for us?'"*

Isaiah replies: *"Here am I. Send me!"*

The Lord calls even today. What is your answer?

Do not let your hands hang limp. *"The Lord your God himself will cross over ahead of you"* (Deuteronomy 31:3).

"...he leads me beside quiet waters" Psalm 23:2

Cell phones can be used to reach others with short text messages far beyond a country's borders. One day during the convention in Hungary, I fell ill. Since my health isn't always on top, I have to be considerate towards it and try to restrict the strain. However, there were so many seminars that I could choose every day, with lecturers of supreme quality, so I participated in too much. One day the rheumatic pains grew so excessive, and I was forced to keep to my bed.

Thinking that I should be lying in my bed all day wasn't at all pleasant. I turned to the Father in prayer about it all.

Then I received a text message from Marit Kjenstad in Froland by Arendal. She knew nothing of my whereabouts or how I was doing, but she wrote that she had been reminded to greet me with Psalm 23:1a-2b: *"The Lord is my shepherd... He leads me beside quiet waters..."*

This gave me peace in my heart, and gratitude for the Father's care for me. He said that He would lead me to rest and strength, that He would give me water and new nourishment.

Far from home, and not feeling well, I was still in the Lord's hands. In Matthew 1:23, it is said about the Lord Jesus Christ: *"The virgin will conceive and give birth to a son, and they will call him Immanuel"* (which means "God with us").

Indeed, *God is with us.* We are never, ever alone.

IN GOD WE TRUST

In God's hand

My book, *In God's Hand,* which I published in 2003, had been published in its third edition when the head of the publishing company, Asbjoern Kvalbein, called and said that he wanted to look into the possibilities of having it published in Sweden and Denmark as well. "Do you know anybody in America who can help you in getting it published there?" he asked. I only knew one lady in the USA. Whether she knew about any publishing company, I didn't know.

"Get in touch with her," he advised me, but I didn't promise anything. I had to pray about it first, I said.

Oeyvind Brakvatne once said: "Be patient and let the Lord open the doors. Be patient and let Him ripen the fruit so that you can go into the works that He has prepared in advance for you. Throughout my life I had some bitter experiences of chances that only I had created, but that God didn't sanction. All of a sudden, I got the open door, the one I thought was open, in my face and unripe fruit in my lap.

"Little by little I've learned to pray far more before entering through the door I thought was open."

This is an important lesson. And so I prayed.

I asked for a sign. Could the Lord send this lady that I knew in the States to Norway to visit me, as a sign that this book should be published over there? And that was all I did. Should this door be opened, then it had to be the Lord alone who opened it.

The biblical meaning of "seven" is perfect, and exactly seven days after this prayer, the lady called me. She had just arrived in Norway, she said. If it was convenient, she would like to visit me this day. She also brought along a friend from America. Would this be okay? Of course it was okay. Indeed, it was my answer to prayer who called.

When they arrived, I told them about Asbjoern's phone call and my prayer to the Lord. I asked whether she knew any publishing company, but *Sorry, no.* Then she turned to her friend, Faye Alden, and asked whether she knew about anyone. She did! Three days later, Faye returned to America with a copy of my book in her suitcase.

Later Faye told me that on the plane she had said to God: "Lord, I'm just a hairdresser. And I know nothing about publishing books. I wish to be your servant in this, but then you must open the doors that need to be opened."

Safely home again, and at work, she told a colleague who was also her interceder about my book. Her interceder advised her to use a different publisher for this book, and gave her his phone number. A little hesitant, she eventually took courage and called him. She knew that the fact that this book only existed in Norwegian could pose a problem – they needed to find someone who could translate it. But the publisher could soon calm her, he had someone who could translate. A month later, the first chapter had been translated, and the publisher called her and said that they wanted to publish this. Faye wrote and kept me up to date about the process. One day, she wrote me this: "God can use us if we are willing. He can even make use of a hairdresser. Because He doesn't call the qualified, but He qualifies those He calls."

This is very true. Just think of the disciples that Jesus called to go with the gospel to the entire world. This has been a great comfort to me. In Zechariah 4:10 it says: *"Who dares despise the day of small things?"* And verse 6 shows us the road to which we are called: *"'Not by might nor by power, but by my Spirit,' says the Lord Almighty."*

The Lord calls, He sends, and He walks together with us. And when the Lord calls, we are given promises at the same time on the way. Just as it says in Deuteronomy 31:8: *"The Lord himself goes before you and will be with you; he will never leave you nor forsake you. Do not be afraid; do not be discouraged."*

We never walk alone on the Lord's road.

Faye Alden was willing to serve with a great heart. She came as a blessing into my life. The title of the American edition of the book became, *In God's Hand*. The first e-mails and greetings from readers have already arrived from the other side of the Atlantic Ocean.

My prayer is such that it is the Lord Jesus that I follow in my walk. For without Him, I can do nothing. I pray as it says in Psalm 86:11: *"Teach me your way, Lord, that I may rely on your faithfulness; give me an undivided heart, that I may fear your name."*

An American Bible

Once, I received a phone call from America with a request whether I could come and preach at some churches there. I replied, saying that I needed to pray about this. I have never had any particular wish to go to the USA. It's a little overwhelming in a way, to think that I should come to America one day. This hasn't been part of my reality. So when I said that I would pray over this, I had no particular thoughts or feelings about it.

When the request came, I was busy with radio broadcasts in connection to a series of meetings in Kristiansand Cathedral. Thus I didn't take the time to pray until a fortnight later.

Later on that evening I said to my husband that we should sit down and pray about what the Lord meant about this whole thing about a trip to America. We prayed that the Lord's will might be done, and that the Lord would grant us means for the trip as a sign that this was a work prepared in advance that He wanted us to walk into.

Early the following morning, before 7:30 a.m. I received a text message from Karl Mosvold in Kristiansand. He had heard that I had been asked to come to America, and now he wanted to give me the financial support I needed for the trip. For days he had been reminded strongly about this.

Thanks were given to God, and of course to the invitation to come and preach. We had prayed late in the evening for advice, and early the next morning the answer came. The following days, the Lord gave several different signs to confirm that we should look at this trip as works prepared in advance.

I had thought that they needed to find an interpreter for me in America, but they said that they didn't need one. The thought made

You are never alone

---

me a little unsure, and I placed the whole thing before God and prayed that He had to let His will be done here, as well. He who sees everything. I didn't feel confident that I mastered the language well enough to stand alone in a pulpit.

When the time closed in, and I realized that there would be no interpreter, I started praying for a Bible in English. I had a New Testament in English, which I had bought in a thrift store, but I didn't have the Old Testament in English. A week before I was going to start on my English sermons, I got a phone call from Farsund. It was Judith Johansen who called. She knew nothing about my approaching trip to America, but she told me that she had been strongly reminded to give me an English Bible. Was I in need of one? "And," she added, "this is the kind they usually use in England, but it is the version that they use in America. There's also some additions in this Bible, since it is a study Bible. It's probably a little worn since I've used it a lot myself, but if you wish, you can get it from me. Do you need such a Bible?"

If I was in need of one? Yes, indeed! I told her about my prayer and my worry concerning me preaching in English. Judith herself had worked almost her entire life with English as her spoken language, and she had heard me talk English when we earlier had been together with a British missionary. Now she told me that I should take it easy regarding the language, it was going to be all right. This helped a little bit, but I felt I needed to turn my gaze upward to Jesus, and at the same time practice and practice speaking English. With the American Bible from the Lord, my courage had risen considerably. He who uses that which is nothing, had gone before me even here.

When we came to America, I was told that my sermons turned out all right. My message had been understood. I thanked the Father.

At some of the places where we held meetings, many people requested intercession and counseling, however, one of the greatest thing I experienced was that four people accepted the Lord Jesus Christ as Lord and savior in a church in Minnesota. The Lord is faithful, when He calls He will also do the work. For it is written: *"The one who calls you is faithful, and he will do it"* (1 Thessalonians 5:24). In this way, He alone received all the glory.

We also experienced that the world isn't as big as we often believe. When I was standing preaching in a church in New York, I told about the Bible I had received as a gift. As I mentioned who had given it to me, an elderly man in the audience flung his arm into the air and shouted in fluent Norwegian: "Det er kusina mi i Farsund!" ("That's my cousin in Farsund!") And so I had a greeting to bring back to Norway as well.

My health wasn't always at its best during my trip, but the Lord went before me. He gave me resting places along the way. On the flight home, I fell ill with fever, and became bedridden a while after my return. This is also a part of my walk with the Lord. But the Lord is faithful, He is always there, every day. For He *"does not change like shifting shadows"* (James 1:17). I'm never alone, whether it is in the pulpit in America, or in my sickbed here at home, or whatever the day may bring. Thus, let us remind each other about what is written in Philippians 4:6: *"Do not be anxious about anything, but in every situation, by prayer and petition, with thanksgiving, present your requests to God."*

I know where I'm going

Interceders are one of life's great blessings. Ellen Lien, an elderly lady in Valle, was one of mine. We had many good conversations while she was still alive. She often told me that when she couldn't fall asleep, she lay awake and prayed into the night. In some of our conversations, we reminded each other of how we should meet again, home with Jesus. We knew where we were going when our journey here on earth was over. It was a blessing for me to know Ellen. Now she has gone home to our Lord Jesus.

When she went, I prayed to Jesus that He had to take good care of her in every way, because I loved her so dearly. I know that everybody receives the best possible treatment and care by Jesus, but it felt good to be able to remind Him about this concerning Ellen. In Psalm 119:19, it says: *"I am a stranger on earth..."* You who read this, do you know where you're going once your time here on earth is over?

You are never alone

One day, as I was working on a sermon about this topic, I received an e-mail from the USA. It was from Faye Alden. As a hairdresser, Faye Alden has done Billy Graham's hair, as well as his wife Ruth's. Now she sent me a story that Billy Graham had experienced and told.

In 2008, Billy Graham was eighty-six years old. He was suffering from Parkinson's disease. In January 2000, leaders in Charlotte, North Carolina, wanted to invite him for a lunch that was going to be held in honor of him alone. However, Billy hesitated to accept this invitation as he was so marked by his disease. They said that they didn't accept a no, he only had to turn up and could sit and simply receive. They just really wanted to make much of him. Billy Graham could do no other than say yes to the invitation.

The day came, and many people said many things to him. When all was said, he himself went up to the platform and said: "Today I was reminded of Albert Einstein, the great physicist who this month has been nominated by *Time Magazine* as the person of the century.

"Einstein once traveled from Princeton by train. The ticket taker came slowly down the aisle in the car checking the passengers' tickets. When he came down to Einstein, Einstein stuck his hand down in the left pocket of his vest, but there was no ticket there. Then he searched the pockets on his pants. It wasn't there either. He opened his suitcase and searched, but neither there was it to be found. He bowed down and searched around his seat, but it was all gone.

"The ticket taker said to him: 'Dr. Einstein, I know who you are. I'm certain that you bought a ticket. Don't worry more about this.' Then he continued down the aisle. Einstein remained seated, shaking his head, somewhat puzzled.

"Just as the ticket taker was passing into the next car, he turned and saw the great physicist crawling on all fours, searching for the ticket under his seat.

"The ticket taker hurried over to him and said: 'Dr. Einstein, Dr. Einstein. Don't worry about this. I know who you are. This is no problem, you don't need the ticket. I'm certain that you bought one.'

"Then Einstein stood up, looked him straight into the eyes and said: 'Young man, I also know perfectly well who I am. On the other hand, what I no longer know since I lost my ticket is where I'm going.'"

When Billy Graham had finished telling this story, he continued by saying: "Do you see the suit I'm wearing today? It is brand new. My wife, my children and my grandchildren keep telling me that I have grown slow on my old days. They tell me I used to be a little more fastidious. So I went out and bought myself a new suit before this lunch and for another occasion. Do you know which occasion that is? This is the suit I want to buried in. But when you hear that I'm gone, I don't want you to remember my suit, but this one thing: I don't just know who I am, but I know where I'm going as well."

I too know this. By grace alone I will go home to the Lord Jesus when this my journey here on earth is over. For it is written in John 3:16: *"For God so loved the world that he gave his one and only Son, that whoever believes in him shall not perish but have eternal life."*

So how does this come about? Well, by faith in the Lord Jesus Christ our life is hidden in Him. His atoning sacrifice on the Calvary cross in our place becomes our ticket to heaven once we accept Him as our Savior. For it is furthermore written in Colossians 3:4: *"When Christ, who is your life, appears, then you also will appear with him in glory."*

It is all so simple and so overwhelming as Paul writes in Romans 10:13: *"Everyone who calls on the name of the Lord will be saved."* Do you know where you're going?

How do you get to heaven?

One day, while I was in Austin, Minnesota, the married couple living in the neighboring house, Audra and Jonathan Baxter, came and knocked on the door. They worked in the Salvation Army and had read my book, *In God's Hand*.

Jonathan said: "But something is lacking in the book. For you haven't written about how one can be saved. You need to include this." I thanked them for this suggestion, and said that I would place this before the Father in prayer. I wanted very much to include a salvation prayer.

Three days later, we were invited home by Betty O'Brien. She had Norwegian ancestors; her grandparents on her father's side were from Nesbyen in Hallingdal, a valley in the southern part of Norway. She had visited Norway, and was very enthusiastic about the country and the people. Betty had also read my book, and now she wondered whether I could use something she had. She had some plastic cards with a salvation prayer on the one side, and a Bible verse on the other. The header was: "How do you get to heaven?"

I was so happy. I told her about my prayer, and about the married couple who had suggested this for my next book. Then she told me that she had become a widow. Her husband, Patrick O'Brien, had died from cancer. Brain tumor. He was a Christian and was on fire for spreading the gospel about the Lord Jesus. Thus he had produced these cards that he handed out. These were made a year before he got ill. When the illness came, he continued to hand them out, as this had grown even more important to him. He lived for twenty-one months after he was diagnosed. When he realized that the end was nearing, he decided that all who came to his funeral should each get one of these cards as a last greeting from him. He himself chose the engraving for his tombstone: *"Whoever will call upon the name of the Lord will be saved"* (Romans 10:13).

The Norwegian professor in theology, Carl Fredrik Wisloeff, said it like this: "There are only two possible exits from this life. One of them is death – the eternal death away from God. The other is eternal life, home with God. Two possibilities: Eternal damnation – eternal salvation. Death is the exit from a life serving sin away from God. Whether these are 'major' sins or 'minor' sins, doesn't really matter. The end is the eternal death. The eternal life is the destination for those who believe in Jesus. No other possibilities than these exist. Those who perish shall forever know within themselves: "This is my own fault. But those who are saved shall praise God and the Lamb for the salvation by mere grace, for Jesus' sake." (From the book *Daglig brød – Daily Bread*)

If you who read this have not yet received Jesus as your Savior in your life, you have the opportunity now. Here are the Bible references and the salvation prayer that were written on Patrick's little card:

Romans 3:10: *"There is no one righteous, not even one..."*
Romans 3:23: *"...for all have sinned and fall short of the glory of God..."*
Romans 5:8: *"...God demonstrates his own love for us in this: While we were still sinners, Christ died for us."*
Romans 5:9: *"Since we have now been justified by his blood, how much more shall we be saved from God's wrath through him!"*
Romans 6:23: *"For the wages of sin is death, but the gift of God is eternal life in Christ Jesus our Lord."*
Romans 8:1: *"Therefore, there is now no condemnation for those who are in Christ Jesus..."*
Romans 10:9: *"If you declare with your mouth, 'Jesus is Lord,' and believe in your heart that God raised him from the dead, you will be saved."*
Romans 10:13: *"Everyone who calls on the name of the Lord will be saved."*

A salvation prayer:

My heavenly Father,
now I come to open my heart
and to receive your promise
in your son Jesus Christ,
for eternal life.

I know that I have sinned.
Forgive me my sins and cleanse me.

I now confess with my mouth
that I now believe in Jesus Christ.

That He died for my sins
and that you rose Him from the dead.

I now receive Jesus Christ
as Lord and Savior in my life.

I know that through the power of His resurrection
in His name
I have forgiveness and eternal life.

I receive this
in the faith of the Lord Jesus Christ.
Amen.

If you now have read this prayer for salvation because you wish to receive the Lord Jesus as your savior, I will say to you with great joy: Welcome as a child of God! Welcome into the family of God! You are now saved.

I encourage you to find a local congregation where you live, and get in touch with them for fellowship and support. You can call the office and ask for the priest or the pastor. Or perhaps you know someone who is a Christian, and whom you trust. Get in touch and tell them this good news.

On your way, I'll give you this:

With joy

With joy
I receive you.

With songs of joy
I lift you up.

With cries of joy
I carry you.

With jubilation
I celebrate
when you
turn around to Me.

And in truth
I lead you.

I am the Lord,
that is my name.
And I
I will rescue and save you.

ABOUT THE AUTHOR

Contact information:
ritaaasen@yahoo.no

Rita Aasen
Andoysloyfen 31
4623 Kristiansand
NORWAY

List of published work (Norwegian titles):

1. **Se Lyset** 1993 – Christian poetry (not translated, unofficial English title "See the Light")
2. **Hør Røsten** 1994 – Christian poetry (not translated, unofficial English title "Hear the Voice")
3. **Gleden i Herren** 1994 – Christian poetry (not translated, unofficial English title "The Delight in the Lord")
4. **Deres styrke** 1994 – Christian poetry (not translated, unofficial English title "Your Strength")
5. **Min nåde er nok** 2002 – Christian poetry (not translated, unofficial English title "My Grace is Sufficient")

These five books have also been published as audiobooks in Norway (2000) through KABB (Kristent Arbeid Blant Blinde og svaksynte = Christian work among blind and visually-impaired people).

Other titles:

6. **Han bærer deg:**
   Everyday life experiences with Jesus. 2003. Four editions. Lunde forlag. ISBN 978-82-520-4792-9.
7. **Du er aldri glemt:**
   Christian poetry, 3 editions. Lunde forlag. ISBN 82-520-4779-3 Reprinted in 2012. (not translated, unofficial English title "You are Never Forgotten")
8. **Du er dyrebar og høyt elsket:** (out of stock)
   Christian poetry. 2005, 2 editions. Lunde forlag ISBN 82-520-4894-3
   (not translated, unofficial English title "You are Precious and Loved")
9. **Tegnet i Guds hender:**
   Christian poetry 2006. Lunde forlag. ISBN 82-520-4938-9 (not translated, unofficial English title "Painted by God's Hand")
10. **Han vandrer foran deg:**
    Christian poetry 2007. Lunde forlag. ISBN 82-520-4985-5 (not translated, unofficial English title "He Walks Before You")
11. * **"In God's hand. Experiencing the Father's Love".**
    Everyday life experiences with Jesus. 2006. ISBN 0-9776713-9-9
12. **Jeg skal ikke forlate deg:**
    Christian poetry 2009. Lunde forlag. ISBN 978-82-520-0077-1 (not translated, unofficial English title "I Will Never Leave you")
13. **Du er aldri alene:**
    Everyday life experiences with Jesus, and Christian poetry 2010. Lunde forlag. ISBN 978-82-520-0124-2. Translated into American English with the title "You are never Alone" *
14. * **"You Are Never Alone".** Translation completed in January 2012. Total word count: 42 144. Ready for publishing.

Rita Aasen is a Norwegian preacher, second leader in Open Doors Norway, author and educated potter. Fifty-five years old, married to Kaare, they have three grown boys. They live in the South of Norway

About the Author

in Kristiansand where she works in a Christian organization – Open Doors, which was founded in the Netherlands by Brother Andrew. They work worldwide now in sixty countries for the persecuted Christian church.

Her calling in life is to testify about the Lord Jesus Christ. Her way of doing this is by writing books, giving speeches, and reaching others through radio and television. Her daily walk with Jesus and trusting completely in Him has given her years and years of experiencing God's constant love and care. She writes about answers to prayer, other people's stories, God in the details, miracles, but also doubt, resistance, tiredness and discouragement. God never promised that we would never face obstacles and difficulties in our everyday lives – but He did promise to never leave us nor forsake us. She wishes to share and make known Our Father's Love for us, and how He sees and hears His children, by sharing her everyday life experiences with Him through an honest and real-life testimony that her work reflects.

She is a Norwegian published author and recently she published a new book in Norway, and upon requests from several Americans had it translated into American English to have it published in the USA.

The book is her twelfth book. The Norwegian title is "Du er aldri alene" and translated into English as "You are never Alone." The original book was published in Norway in 2010 by publisher Lunde Forlag AS (www.lundeforlag.no).

Her best-selling books inform the publishing house Lunde in Norway. All the stories are real life stories. Everyday life experiences with Jesus. She has received many feedbacks through the years that Jesus has touched people through these books.